THIMBLES
of
AUSTRALIA

Sue Gowan started collecting thimbles in 1984 when she was given a Wedgwood thimble, commemorating Wedgwood's 250th anniversary, by her husband. This has led to a love for and fascination in learning more about these sewing tools. Many collectors come to thimble collecting through using a thimble, but Sue has never sewed.

She was an early member of the Thimble Collectors Club of South Africa, from 1985 until she moved to live in Australia in 1988. She joined both the Thimble Society of London and Thimble Collectors International (TCI) in 1985, the Needlework Tool Collectors Society of Australia in 1988 and the Dorset Thimble Society in 1994. The local group of thimble collectors in Brisbane is now her grass roots contact with other collectors.

Sue has attended many thimble conventions throughout the world. These include a thimble convention in South Africa in 1990; the four Corroborees held by the Needlework Tool Collectors Society of Australia in Melbourne in 1990, 1992, 1994 and 1996; and she was fortunate enough to be at the Dorset Thimble Society's 10th anniversary conference in Southampton in 1995.

In June 1987, Sue started Thimbleselect, her mail order thimble business, in South Africa, in response to the dearth of locally available thimbles and a desire to get other people interested in collecting thimbles. The business moved with her when she settled in Perth in 1988 and continues today in Brisbane, where she's known as the 'thimble lady' at collectors' fairs throughout south-east Queensland. Many of the thimbles mentioned in the book are available through Thimbleselect.

In 1995, Sue privately published *Thimbles and other Needlework Tools: a selective bibliography*, a 200 page, 1200 entry research tool; copies have sold all over the world. This has enabled her to build up an extensive thimble library. Her personal thimble collection is wildly eclectic, having grown mainly through exchanging thimbles with other collectors worldwide. Her passion for Australian thimbles makes for exciting hunting.

Sue is a librarian for a firm of engineering consultants and is an avid reader. She is married to Mike and has two adult children, Richard and Christie.

Betty Maloney is the well known author and botanical artist. Betty received her first thimble, a Dorcas in its box, for her 21st birthday but it was not until 1964 that she began to search out thimbles—at that time St Vincent de Paul shops had silver thimbles for 6d each! After she had brought home a few, her husband Reg informed her that if there were any more thimbles he'd be leaving home. 'I'll miss you' was the response from one of Australia's first thimble collectors! Betty has been a long-time member of the Thimble Society of London and more recently the Needlework Tool Collectors Society of Australia.

Betty Maloney was born in Colac, Victoria. She trained in art at the RMIT and taught at Melbourne Church of England Girls Grammar School and St Catherine's before marrying and moving to Sydney. She became interested in native flora and began botanical illustrating in 1964. She co-authored *Designing Australian Bush Gardens* and *More About Bush Gardens* with her sister Jean Walker. Betty's own bush garden is classified by the National Trust.

The Proteaceae of the Sydney Region with Alec Blombery (Angus & Robertson, limited edition, 1981) has been her largest undertaking, involving 86 water colour paintings. These paintings, together with a further 96 paintings of fruits of the Proteaceae and all the preliminary drawings, have been acquired by the State Library of New South Wales.

THIMBLES
of
AUSTRALIA

INCLUDING THIMBLES OF THE WORLD
WITH AN AUSTRALIAN CONNECTION

Susan Jean Gowan

with illustrations by Betty Maloney

Kangaroo Press

Dedicated to
Michael, Richard and Christie

National Library of Australia
Cataloguing-in-Publication data:

Thimbles of Australia: including thimbles of the world
with an Australian connection.

Bibliography.
Includes index.
ISBN 0 86417 949 4.

1. Thimbles - Australia. I. Gowan, Susan Jean. II. Title.

646.19

Design: Wing Ping Tong
Photography: Susan Jean Gowan and others as credited

© Susan Jean Gowan 1998

This work is copyright. Apart from any use permitted under the Copyright Act, no part may be reproduced by any process, or any other exclusive right exercised, without the permission of Susan Jean Gowan.

First published in 1998 by Kangaroo Press Pty Ltd
An imprint of Simon & Schuster Australia
20 Barcoo Street (PO Box 507) East Roseville 2069 NSW Australia

Printed in Singapore by Colour Symphony

ISBN 0 86417 946 4

Contents

Preface 6
Acknowledgments 8
Locations of thimble makers in Australia 9
Glossary 10
Introduction 11

Silver Thimbles 15
1900–1950 16
1950— 32
Commemorative thimbles 41
Other silver thimbles 42

Gold Thimbles 43

China and Porcelain Thimbles 48
Handpainted thimbles 59
Breaddough-on-porcelain thimbles 61
Pottery thimbles 62
Unbranded china thimbles 64

Metal Thimbles 67
Aluminium thimbles 67
Brass thimbles 74
Copper thimbles 76
Enamel thimbles 77
Metal thimbles 77
Pewter thimbles 78
Silver-plated thimbles 82
Thimblefuls 83

Wooden Thimbles 85

Other Thimbles 91
Crystal and glass thimbles 91
Horn and bone thimbles 91
Ivory thimbles 92
Leather thimbles 93
Natural fibre thimbles 94
Papier-mâché thimbles 95
Plant material thimbles 95
Plastic thimbles 96
Shell thimbles 99
Stone thimbles 99
Sewing kits 100
Miscellaneous 101

Thimble Boxes and Thimble Holders 102
Porcelain thimble holders 102
Australian jewellers' thimble boxes 102

Appendix 1 Australian thimble marks 106
Appendix 2 Koalas on thimbles 109
Appendix 3 China painters and woodturners 115
Appendix 4 Pan Arts china thimbles 116
Appendix 5 Advertisements and Gibson's patent 118
Appendix 6 Chronology of jewellers, silversmiths and china manufacturers 126
Bibliography 128
Useful addresses 130
Index 131

Preface

In 1984, when I paid my initial visit to the Thimble Society of London, I bought my first Australian thimble. It was one of the papier-mâché thimbles by Haley. I remember at the time being most impressed by the unknown Australians who had gone to the lengths of having thimbles sold in London. From then on, I actively sought out Australian thimbles through penfriends and contact with the mail order businesses of the day. Barbara Kelly of Newcastle in New South Wales particularly made an impression on me by the way she so actively promoted Australian thimbles. I never dreamt I too would one day be an Australian.

Once I was living in Australia the hunt for thimbles began in earnest and nowadays the Australian component of my thimble collection is the largest. I battled to find information on Australian thimbles and so I was delighted when Iris Woolley wrote two articles devoted exclusively to them. These articles, that appeared in the *TCI Bulletin* and *Thimble Notes and News* in 1988, were never available to the general collecting public of Australia. I wanted as many people as possible to know the history of Australian thimbles and thus the idea of the book was born.

In thinking about the scope of this book, I decided to include all thimbles relating to Australia, whether made in Australia or overseas. Without the overseas component the scope for study would have been very limited and the book would have been pamphlet-sized. I have included all the thimbles mentioned by Iris Woolley in her original articles.

I have arranged the chapters according to what the thimbles are principally made of, rather than by category. Thimbles produced in Australia and those from overseas are mixed in alphabetical sequence by thimblemaker in each section.

The themes of the thimbles can be accessed through the comprehensive index, e.g. commemorative thimbles, advertising thimbles and souvenir thimbles, or by the town or the state where the thimbles are made. With a relatively small range of thimbles available in Australia, compared to say England or the United States, it has been relatively easy to include specific details of special commissions for collectors to follow. A chronology of Australian thimble dates is given in Appendix 6.

To appeal to as wide a cross-section of thimble collectors as possible, every known type of thimble of Australia has been included—from the early gold and silver highly collectable thimbles, through the 'cheap and cheerful' range of china, the novelty, the gimmicky, to the handmade thimbles of today. The current thimble industry is too young for me to be discriminatory at this stage. In the modern silver section as many silversmiths as possible have been included for future reference. With one exception, thimbles held in Australian museums and historic homes have not been included. From an earlier survey of museums by Nerylla Taunton, very few, if any, of the needlework tools, including thimbles, are Australian made: only their provenance is Australian.

Thimbles from both commercial factory production and from studios have been included. It should be noted that manufacturers of thimbles in the twentieth century did not make thimbles as their principal output. They were jewellers and china manufacturers first, with thimbles forming a fraction of their production.

There are many books specifically written about the overseas silver and bone china thimble manufacturers, so I have included only a brief outline on these makers where relevant to Australian thimbles. There are no illustrations of their backstamps. Otherwise, I have included as much physical detail as possible in the description of each thimble, as one cannot always capture the band,

Preface

the marks and the apex in a photograph. It is only by close inspection of every aspect of each thimble in a collection, and by comparison with similar thimbles, that one learns anything new. To appreciate the many aspects of thimbles, it is necessary to look at details, such as where the thimble is indented and what maker's marks are present, including china backstamps and so on. These are the sorts of details that should be recorded in a collector's catalogue. My task of description has often been made easier by referring to the leaflet that accompanied the thimble at the time of purchase.

In compiling this book for collectors of thimbles, it is hoped that many previously unrecognised thimbles will be able to be identified as Australian ones. This in turn could lead to a hunt for other Australian thimbles. If it does, this whole project will have been worthwhile.

Over 250 photographs have been included to help in identification, and the illustrations of maker's marks by Betty Maloney are an added descriptive tool. Many of the maker's marks have worn badly over the years or been poorly struck and it is the skill of Betty's pen that has brought them to life. There is a listing of maker's marks in Appendix 1.

It has been a difficult task to choose which photos to include to best illustrate the salient points of each type of thimble. With the hundreds of modern Australian china thimbles available to choose from, any photographic omission from this book in no way reflects on their collectability. The choice of which colour photographs to include was quite arbitrary and does not reflect the desirability or importance of the thimble, though gold thimbles do look better in colour.

I have included the quantity of thimbles made where this is known. I feel it helps to establish a complete picture of the availability and rarity, or otherwise, of the thimbles being described. Of course, the number made is often dictated by the firm supplying the thimbles and in some cases is far in excess of demand.

Having accumulated a large thimble library, I have been able to include any references to Australian thimbles wherever they have appeared in the literature; the range of reference is surprisingly wide.

It is difficult to give advice on which thimbles to collect. A thimble collection is a very personal and private one and reflects the interests and passions of each individual. One should buy what appeals and establish small pockets of speciality items that one is passionate about that add to the thrill of the chase. There are enough trails to follow up on in the pages of this book. Some people collect thimbles because they are fascinated by sewing tools from an earlier era and are attracted to thimbles that have been used for sewing. Others are attracted to a theme, for example flowers. One collector in the United States has a specialist collection based on violets, and has amassed around 100 thimbles with this theme. Themes in Australia might include State flowers, for example waratahs. Appendix 2 demonstrates a selection of thimbles with koalas. There are also different types of thimbles to collect, such as thimblefuls, or thimbles by a particular maker or in a specific medium, all of which would make a good niche collection.

Once you commit to thimble collecting, you will have joined one of the fastest growing areas of collecting in the world. Digitabulists (as thimble collectors are known) are the fourth largest group behind doll, stamp and coin collectors. There are thimble societies to join and mail order concerns to contact, so start by fossicking through the workboxes that have been handed down through the family—here you will find the thimbles to treasure and to get to know more about. The thimbles available in Australia range in price from $1.00 through to hundreds of dollars.

One of the favourite sayings of Bridget McConnell, of the Thimble Society of London, is 'Thimble collectors might be considered frivolous but it is always undertaken by serious people.'

There will be omissions in such a new field of research and I welcome comments of any sort. Any errors are my responsibility alone.

Sue Gowan
Brisbane
January 1998

Acknowledgments

This book would not have been possible without the thimble collectors of Australia and even beyond. No one collector can hope to have every Australian thimble in their collection. When I approached them, collectors willingly surveyed their collections for Australian thimbles for me and were often most surprised at the variety represented there. They opened up their collections to me to photograph and generously shared their knowledge and gave encouragement and hospitality at every turn. They even sent me their thimbles to photograph! There has been support and help from the wider community as well, in response to my newspaper appeals.

I would love to thank everyone for all the help I have received. My thanks go to the following people; they will know what contribution they gave—it is greatly appreciated. This listing may seem a little 'bald' but it is done deliberately to protect the anonymity of the thimble collectors listed amongst the following:

Nelda Anders, Dorothy Andrews, Judy Andrews, staff of the Australian Industrial Property Organisation in Brisbane and Melbourne, Irene Barnett, Lee Bateman, Shirley Bennett, Glenda Beverley, Clarice and Dave Birch, Joan Blythe, Wendy Brittain, Patricia Brown, Joy Bull of the Wedgwood Collectors Society, Helen Burgin, Sue Caesar, Mena Carroll, Sue Christensen, Jeannie Chryn, Dorothy Collins, Yvonne and Des Coote, Beryl Crago, Nancye Crooks, Helen Cunningham, Brenda Dean, Lynn Dennis, Eve Dickson, Nance Dunne, Margaret Dyne, Miep van Eijk, The Embroiderers Guild NSW, The Embroiderers Guild of South Australia Inc, Val Field, Margaret Frecker, Fay Griffiths, Gallery One Thimbles, Adrian Graham-Rowe, Pat Gray, Sybil Harland, Sally Hearn, Margaret Henriksen, Robert Herron, Beryl Hewitt, Margaret Hickling, Curtis Hine, Pat Holcombe, Nigel Holmes of The Gap Photography Centre, Val Hoskin, Peggy Jardine, Di and Simon Jura, Barbara Kelly, Jim Kirkpatrick, Ian and Betty Lauder, Betty and Reg Maloney, R.P.A. Matho-Dudare, Shirley and Charles McPhee, Betty McPhie, Sandra Menger, Pat Meppem, Lola Moate, Gwen Moore, Needlework Tool Collectors Society of Australia Inc, Pan Arts Importing, Joyce Nixon-Smith, Joan Nock, Lois O'Sullivan, Nola Pank, Jane Peek of the Australian War Memorial, Di Pelham Burn, Lee Perry, Joy and Chris Pitts, John and Nancy Read of Top Rockz Gallery, Edna Reid, Lynn Richards, Wendy Ritchie, Craig Rolley-Good of Mr B the Optometrist, Norma Shattock, Frank Shorter, Ann and Bernard Shuttleworth, Tricia Smout, Myra Stanbury of the Western Australian Maritime Museum, staff of the Mitchell Library of the State Library of New South Wales, staff of the State Library of Victoria, Sturt Craft Centre, Margaret Sutton, Tamrookum Valley Craft, Thimble Society of London, Nerylla Taunton, Margaret Towler, Jack Turner, Dick and Ann Wallace, Col Ward, Beryl and Graham Warne, Pauline Watts, Westminster China, Sue and Roger Wilson, Yvonne Winspear, Iris Woolley.

Iris Woolley wrote the first articles on Australian thimbles and my inspiration and motivation must be attributed to her.

Helen Burgin provided written information on modern Australian thimbles, which was invaluable. Ann Wallace made available her notes entitled 'Thimbles galore'.

Her attention to detail, her natural talent as an artist and her love of thimbles have made it a pleasure to work with Betty Maloney.

Wendy Ritchie deserves a special vote of thanks for her expert opinion in the reading of the manuscript.

Acknowledgments

My daughter Christie Gowan, Joyce Nixon-Smith and Betty Maloney helped with constructive criticism in the reading of the manuscript.

For permission to reproduce photographs and advertisements, I am indebted to the Western Australian Maritime Museum (page 11), Meadow Lea Foods (page 73), John Hawkins (page 20), and Mr B the Optometrist (page 71).

A note on cross-referencing
The word *Plate* in italics, plus a number, refers to a colour plate; the letter K plus a number in parentheses, e.g. (K6), refers to a photograph in Appendix 2: Koalas on thimbles.

LOCATIONS OF THIMBLEMAKERS IN AUSTRALIA

Glossary

Acanthus Leaf like decoration on thimbles. Ornamental use of the acanthus plant has been known since ancient Greek times

Apex The top of the thimble, both inside and out

Backstamp The term applied to the maker's mark stamped inside china and porcelain thimbles

Band The area above the rim—it is usual to find maker's marks on sterling silver thimbles on the band

Cartouche A blank area in an oval, oblong or shield shape on silver or gold thimbles specifically designed for engraving of initials, names, dates or inscriptions

Decal A transfer applied to a thimble. Decals are fired onto glazed china thimbles. Under a magnifying glass a decal can be seen as hundreds of dots. Handpainted thimbles do not show dots

Guilloche The effect on enamel thimbles. The silver underneath the translucent enamel is engine turned with very fine ribbing to give a better surface for the application of enamel

Indentations These are the dimples all over a thimble or on the apex that prevent the needle from slipping whilst sewing. Also known as knurling, dimpling or grating

Lozenge The term applied to the punch of the silver hallmark in which the lettering is placed—it is usually oblong in shape and can have the corners truncated

Patent Deals with the construction and design of the thimble

Registered number Deals with the pattern on the thimble

Rim The edge of the thimble. Also known as the collar

Rolled The rim of the thimble has been turned or folded

Scrimshaw Carving or engraving of intricate designs and patterns on ivory or bone.

Stippled Engraved by using small dots

Verso On the opposite side—usually the back

Introduction

Thimbles have been used in the shape and form that we know today since the fourteenth century. They are made to wear on the end of the finger to help apply pressure on the needle whilst sewing and to protect the tip of the finger.

Australia is a vast country that was only settled 210 years ago. The population of nearly 18 million live mainly around the coastal areas of the continent, concentrated around the capital cities in each of the six states and two territories. Being such a young country, without the thimble history or the population of Europe or America, little thimble archaeological history exists in Australia. Thimbles have only been made in Australia since around 1900.

It is estimated that between 300 000 and 500 000 Aborigines lived in Australia at the time of European settlement, having been here for the last 60 000 years. Before contact with Europeans, Aborigines in the southern half of Australia would have used cloaks and rugs of possum and kangaroo skins, sewn or laced together, against the cold winters. According to Flood (1980) 'these skins would have been stitched together with thread from the long tendons of the muscles about the tail of the kangaroo ... the needle formed from a piece of bone', or from fish bones. Flood also lists the sewing aids that would have been used in producing these cloaks and these were of natural materials, such as shells and small stones, used for preparing the skins. In Europe thimbles had only become necessary when steel needles were introduced. As the Aborigines used bone for needles, thimbles would not have been essential.

Technically the first thimbles in Australia were those from shipwrecks. During the seventeenth and eighteenth centuries, four ships of the Dutch East India Company were wrecked off the Western Australian coast, long before European settlement began in 1788. The remains of the *Batavia*, wrecked on the Abrolhos Islands in 1629, were discovered in the late 1960s. Artefacts and a section of the stern raised from 1971 onwards are on display at the Western Australian Maritime Museum in Fremantle.

Edwin Holmes, in an article in the *TCI Bulletin* of July 1986 on thimbles found on shipwrecks, first drew thimble collectors' attention to one of the thimbles found on the *Batavia*. The Department of Maritime Archaeology of the Maritime Museum in Fremantle has confirmed that the thimble illustrated in this article is in fact from the 1727 wreck of the *Zeewijk*. Two other thimbles from the *Zeewijk* are on display at the Museum's regional museum in Geraldton, Western Australia. There are two thimbles, however, that were raised from the *Batavia* in 1971. They comprise part of the collection assigned to the Commonwealth of Australia and the Netherlands, so are not on display in Fremantle. The Netherlands was the principal source of thimbles in the seventeenth century and these Dutch brass thimbles that have been salvaged from the wrecks are a link with those seventeenth century seamen. They are open-ended thimbles, though the thimble illustrated, from the *Batavia*, may have had an apex.

Australia was first sighted by Captain James Cook on the *Endeavour* on 29 April 1770. Eighteen years later, in 1788, Captain Arthur Phillip brought the First Fleet from Britain. The fleet included 211 marines and 736 convicts.

Seventeenth century Dutch brass thimble from the wreck of the Batavia. *Photo by Patrick Baker, courtesy of the WA Maritime Museum*

From those first small beginnings, a vibrant nation was born.

It is noteworthy that two convicts were sentenced to fourteen years' transportation to Australia for the stealing of a thimble! Catherine Steel and Johanna Brown were indicted for stealing, amongst other items from a reticule, a thimble from Jane Welby in London. Another convict, Mary Adams, was transported on the *Lady Penrhyn* in the First Fleet for seven years for stealing a silver thimble. Elizabeth Fry, the renowned prison reformer, arranged for women convicts on leaving England to be given the patches, needles and thread required for making patchwork quilts on the voyage to Australia.

As the settlement developed free immigrants arrived, as did the families of convicts who had earned their freedom. The new settlers were from all backgrounds and intent on making a life in their new land. Thimbles, treasured possessions produced by nineteenth century British silversmiths and brassmakers, would have been brought with the new migrants. All girls and women of that era would have had to be able to sew as a necessity. This included sewing all the family's clothing and the household bedding and linen and the thimble, so vital for long hours of handsewing, would have seen many hours of service. During the nineteenth century there would have been much mending, remaking and reworking of precious fabric. De Vries-Evans (1987) quotes from Fanny Bussell, a pioneer of Western Australia: 'needles . . . buttons . . . are of the greatest value. We used to wear out our thimbles very quickly when we have so much to sew'. Mary Gilmore (1986) gives a delightful insight into life at the turn of the century: 'there was a time when thimbles, scissors, needles and pins were nursed and minded as though they were treasures . . . I have seen . . . a woman who had for a thimble an open topped strip of hide that went round her thumb like a sailor's or a tailor's thimble'.

The sewing machine was invented in the 1850s and reached women of the Australian bush in the 1860s. The rural and country women of Australia during the nineteenth century depended on hawkers or peddlers and the regular arrival of merchants such as the Myer brothers in country Victoria. They would have been eagerly anticipated for the supply of haberdashery items including thimbles. According to De Vries-Evans (1987) Georgina McCrae, a miniature painter in Melbourne in the 1840s, is described as follows: 'the only thing to cheer her up was the arrival of a box . . . sent from England . . . cotton, needles and pins, all difficult to obtain in early colonial Australia'.

During the nineteenth century, tailoresses were in demand especially on the country properties. They would be hired to spend up to six weeks at a time with the family making all the family clothes required for the season. Though most women would have had little time for decorative needlework, the more well-to-do would have sewn for pleasure by doing fine needlework.

In 1990 a number of nineteenth century brass thimbles were unearthed during an archaeological project prior to the redevelopment of a building site in Melbourne. This is of special interest to thimble collectors in that the site is known to have been occupied by tailors and milliners.

Thimbles from Mesopotamia found their way to Australia after World War I, when many returning soldiers brought back silver niello thimbles, made by the Marsh Arabs, as souvenirs for their wives, mothers, sisters or sweethearts. These thimbles remain in families around the country as treasured possessions. In niello work the silversmith makes a black metal alloy of sulphides of silver, copper and lead and fuses this enamel-like mixture into an engraved area on the thimble. The surface is then polished flat, leaving the black design associated with niello work. The engraved designs are local scenes of the area and include sailing boats, camels and palm trees. Each design is different. These thimbles are still being made today, so it is the thimbles with a provenance of an Australian soldier from World War I that are most sought after.

Until the 1940s and early 1950s tortoiseshell plastic fingerguards were used in schools in Australia, where girls were taught to use thimbles whilst sewing. These guards were worn on the index finger of the left hand. Most children nowadays have never seen a thimble used, never

Silver niello Mesopotamian thimble from Baghdad 1918

Introduction

mind knowing how to use one. Thimbles were produced in Australia until the late 1940s and in this period were made solely for use as sewing tools.

In the 1950s, ready to wear clothing became widely available and sewing went out of fashion. No thimbles were produced in the 1950s and 1960s in Australia, a situation reflected in the rest of the world, where thimble manufacturers experienced great difficulties. Before these accessories of a passing era could sink into oblivion, people started to collect them. Thimble collecting started in earnest all over the world during the 1970s and has led to a revival in thimble making, though from this time onwards thimbles were made mainly for the collectables market. Thimble collecting started in Australia in the 1960s with one or two collectors. The 1970s and 1980s saw thimble collecting grow considerably.

The number of countries that have produced modern thimbles for the Australian market reads like a gazetteer; very few thimbles have been made entirely in Australia and those that have should be treasured. Countries as close as New Zealand and Indonesia, those as far away as Austria, Germany, Portugal, Wales and across to the United States, China, Taiwan and Japan, have all produced thimbles with an Australian theme. England still dominates as the principal supplier of Australian thimbles for the Australian market, as it did at the turn of the century. Most of the large and well known English china manufacturers, including Royal Worcester and Wedgwood, made Australiana thimbles.

Australia has flora and fauna unique to this continent, koalas and kangaroos being amongst our best known icons. Their portraits are the most widespread design themes found on thimbles. Living in Australia one tends to become blasé about these creatures, but as thimble designs they are eminently collectable by visitors to the country. Drawing on the local flora and fauna, artists and thimblemakers have capitalised on this uniqueness and modern Australian thimbles reflect the diversity of the country.

With a good supply of modern Australian silver thimbles available, an attractive niche collection can be assembled, as thimbles in this section are the antiques of the future. There is a growing awareness of and demand for wholly Australian made thimbles and craftspeople can take heart from this phenomenon. Demand for quality, locally made thimbles comes from both the domestic and overseas traveller.

As thimble collecting became popular in Australia, various businesses opened which specialise in thimbles and sewing tools.

Nerylla Taunton is the doyenne of thimble and needlework accessories in Australia. Nerylla opened her Sydney shop, Nerylla's Antiques, in 1977, selling top quality antique sewing tools; after twenty years hers is the only business in Australia devoted solely to sewing accessories, attracting collectors from around Australia and abroad. Nerylla is sought after as a world class expert on all forms of sewing tools. She has written numerous articles on thimbles and needlework tools for several leading craft and antique magazines in Australia. She is the co-author of *Chatelaines* (1995), and her *Antique needlework tools and the embroideries* was published in 1997.

Beryl Warne, a thimble collector in Melbourne, opened her thimble shop, Thimble Collections, in Toorak in 1983. This treasure trove attracted thimble collectors from all over Australia and overseas. Beryl actively sought out local thimble makers from whom she commissioned thimbles for Thimble Collections, and had several buying trips abroad. After three years of highly successful trading, with redevelopment looming, Beryl sold her business to Margaret and Jihl Berry of Mt Eliza in Victoria. The Berrys operated Thimble Collections by mail order and briefly had a thimble stall in the Camberwell Antique Market in Melbourne. In 1990 the Berrys sold off their stock, thus ending a seven year, top quality thimble business.

In 1985 Yvonne Varey started retailing thimbles under the name Gallery One in Western Australia. Her thimble-sized stall in the Fremantle Markets was a mecca for thimble collectors. Gallery One ventured into the wholesale thimble business in 1989 in Perth and mainly sources thimbles from England with an Australian theme. This has progressed to finding Australians to make Australian thimbles. Nowadays Yvonne's trading name is Gallery One Thimbles and she is based in Melbourne.

Barbara Kelly, who ran a successful thimble shop in Hamilton in Newcastle from 1986, started the first thimble newsletter in Australia—this was as a mail order business known as The Thimble Collector. Barbara closed her shop in 1988, but continued selling thimbles by mail order, concentrating on Australian thimbles. She attracted the attention of thimble collectors worldwide through her advertisements in *Thimble Exchange Circle*, published in England, and *Thimble Society of London*. Through The Thimble Collector it became easier for collectors overseas to acquire Australian thimbles without ever having visited Australia. Barbara has written articles on thimbles that have appeared in thimble society magazines all around the world. After a brief stay in the Woollahra Antiques Centre in Sydney, Barbara sent out her last catalogue in 1993, but she will shortly resume selling thimbles.

Sue Gowan brought her mail order business, Thimbleselect, with her from South Africa in 1988. She operated initially in Perth and now serves south-east Queensland, selling modern thimbles at collectors' fairs. Her mail order business caters for collectors all around Australia. More recently Sue has specialised in selling part or entire thimble and needlework tool collections.

Dorothy Andrews has run Thimbella from her home in Meadows near Adelaide since 1985. As the name suggests, Dot sells thimbles and bells—by mail order, at fairs around South Australia and from her Paris Creek Pottery. Thimbella has commissioned thimbles to their own designs which have been widely distributed through retail outlets in South Australia.

Helen Burgin, through her mail order thimble business Addaline Miniatures was the outlet for modern Australian thimbles during the 1980s. Helen has not actively sold thimbles since 1994.

As thimble collecting grew in Australia the need arose for a society for collectors. In July 1987 the first meeting of the Needlework Tool Collectors Society of Australia took place in Melbourne. The idea was first conceived by Nancye Crooks and advertised in *Thimble Exchange Circle* in 1986. Owing to Nancye's ill health, Jenny and Katrina Cowen got the group off the ground; they were Secretary and Chairperson for seven years, leading the Society from strength to strength. The Society has met since 1987, roughly eight times a year in school or local halls. A newsletter has appeared after every meeting since the Society's inception.

The Society's first convention, known as a Corroboree, was held in 1990 in Melbourne and conventions have been held biennially ever since. These conferences have included many expert speakers and the sales malls are an important feature. They are also an excellent opportunity for country and interstate members to travel to Melbourne for a weekend of sharing. As the name suggests, thimble collectors only form a proportion of the membership.

From an initial membership of five the Society now averages a membership of over 110 and though based in Melbourne this number includes members from all around Australia and overseas. The Society became incorporated in 1994. Informal groups spawned through the Society operate in Sydney, Adelaide and Brisbane.

In 1988 Jack Turner started a thimble group for collectors in Adelaide. The group is known as SADS (South Australian Digitabulists Society). The membership averages 25 to 30 and this informal group meets in members' homes five times a year. Membership is not confined to Adelaide collectors and SADS even has one international member. There are handpainted Society thimbles for members and a newsletter has appeared since the inception of the Society.

Pan Arts, the largest thimble wholesalers in Australia, have ensured that Australian thimbles have reached the widest possible market, including overseas, by using The Thimble Guild in Scotland, one of the largest mail order thimble businesses worldwide, to distribute their range of thimbles. The Thimble Guild was previously known as Scotland Direct and Thimble Collectors Guild.

Mention should also be made of the Thimble Society of London. A quality catalogue has been issued quarterly since 1981; it contains hundreds of photographs of thimbles both old and modern for sale and is an excellent guide to current prices. It is widely read in the 'small world of thimbles'. Australian thimbles have appeared in these catalogues over the years.

Silver thimbles

Silver thimbles were made in huge quantities in England, Germany and the United States during the nineteenth century. In England, from around 1884 all silver thimbles had to be hallmarked. Before this date the weight of a thimble had been considered too small to warrant hallmarking. Sterling silver consists of .925 parts of pure silver and .075 parts alloy. European silver has a lower content of silver: .800 parts. A word on the British hallmarking system is needed here. The hallmark guarantees the use of sterling silver, indicated by the symbol of a lion. There are several assay offices which each has its own symbol forming the second part of the hallmark. The third part is an alphabetic symbol signifying the year the item was assayed. In the early years of this century, each assay office changed its date letter at different times of the year: Birmingham, represented by an anchor, changed every June, for example, and Chester, represented by three wheat sheaves and a sword, changed every July. Besides these hallmarks, maker's marks and size marks are to be found on thimbles. Maker's marks are vitally important to the thimble collector today for identification. It is also quite usual for thimbles made in England by the four big thimble manufacturers (Griffith, Fenton, Swann and Horner) at the turn of this century to be marked with the initials of wholesalers instead of their own.

Silversmiths from all over the world have settled in Australia. A small number, working for the large jewellery firms in Melbourne and Sydney in the early twentieth century, made thimbles, but never in large quantities. The jewellery quarter in Melbourne was situated in Little Collins Street between Swanston and Elizabeth Streets, a flourishing area until World War II.

The names of Nifty and Elfin dominate the Australian-manufactured thimble arena and are the most sought after Australian silver thimbles. For anyone hazarding a guess on which of these two makers are better represented in thimble collections around Australia today, more Elfin thimbles have survived and found their way into collections than Nifty thimbles.

Parallel with the burgeoning numbers of Australian made thimbles, large numbers of English silver thimbles were imported into Australia, complete with hallmarks. These thimbles then had the selling jeweller's name, as a form of advertising, added in Australia. There is no evidence that silver thimbles were imported into Australia from England without hallmarks, to have Australian marks struck on.

Thimbles made of sterling silver are prone to go to holes with long use, and once a thimble has a hole in it, the needle will always find that hole, making the thimble difficult to use for sewing. Charles Horner's Dorcas thimble, first patented in England in 1884, overcame this problem. Dorcas thimbles are made of a steel core, with a layer of silver both inside and outside making them virtually indestructible. They still have the beauty of a silver thimble but are more practical for sewing. Lassetter's, Stewart Dawson & Co. and Anthony Hordern were three Sydney firms which imported Dorcas thimbles from around the turn of the century. Dorcas thimbles ceased to be manufactured in England in 1947, but they were actively advertised in the 1950s in Australia and were still for sale into the 1970s. A magnet will always attract a Dorcas thimble. Steel-cored silver thimbles have also been made in Australia.

Silver thimble sizing is not uniform and it is a question of economics that determines the other factor of sizing—the range of sizes made by a particular manufacturer. The large English silver thimble manufacturers differed in the manner of their sizing as well as in the number of available sizes. Henry Griffith and James Fenton used a system where the higher the size number, the larger the thimble, whereas Charles Horner and James Swann used the opposite. The Australian silver thimble sizing diverged as well: Nifty thimbles were sized between 6 and 10 and Elfin between sizes 2 and 6. They were, however, consistent in that the higher the number, the smaller the thimble.

Modern Australian silversmiths such as Curtis Hine and Pat Hagan have realised the significance of sizing their thimbles and having a range of sizes available.

1900–1950

The Commonwealth of Australia came into being with Federation in January 1901 and from this time onwards silver thimbles began to be made in Australia. One of the reasons for this was the Trade Act. The new Commonwealth Government introduced tariffs on a variety of imported goods, including jewellery, and firms which had previously imported jewellery and silverware from England, Europe and America turned to making their own.

There is no established hallmarking of silver in Australia as there is in the United Kingdom. From the early 1900s through to the 1920s though, a system of marking of silver items was introduced by the jewellery associations in Sydney and Melbourne.

The Manufacturing Jewellers' Association of Victoria, formed in 1889, adopted a set of standards for the quality of goods made by its members. Pieces of jewellery would be stamped with guaranteed quality marks and the registered mark of the jeweller. Marks of six Victorian jewellers were registered throughout the Commonwealth of Australia from 1903. In 1920 there were 36 jewellers in Victoria using registered marks but the number had dwindled to 20 by 1942.

The Sydney Hall Mark Company was registered in 1916 but it was only in 1920 that jewellers took the unanimous decision to adopt the principle of hallmarking. The silver mark adopted in New South Wales was a wren—this stamp was to be accompanied by the mark for silver and the maker's mark and the year date letter. The year lettering began with A in 1923. The marks were intended to be self regulated by the jewellery trade. The system unfortunately did not outlive World War II in Victoria and New South Wales and no hallmarking

SILVER THIMBLES

legislation was ever introduced on a federal level in Australia.

Sadly, no known silver thimbles exist bearing any of the New South Wales silver hallmarks from the 1920s. The accompanying reproduction from the *Commonwealth Jeweller and Watchmaker* lists all the Sydney and Melbourne jewellers who used the new standardised marks in 1924.

South Australia, where a number of Germans settled in the nineteenth century, had a significant number of German silversmiths and jewellers. Some of the finest silverware in Australia was made in Adelaide last century. No system of marking was used in South Australia.

The most common way of identifying the quality of silver thimbles made in Australia in this period is the use of the abbreviations 'Stl Sil', 'Stg Silver' or 'St S'.

In 1985 Marian Lipsius, an American thimble collector, visited Australia. On her return to California, a report of her visit appeared in the *Southern Californian Thimble Collectors*. In her account Marian reported that William Kerr of Sydney, Prouds of Sydney and Thomas Stokes of Melbourne—all jewellers at the turn of the century— were reputed to have made thimbles. Stokes were very large manufacturing jewellers, specialising in teaspoons and enamel badges for the souvenir market, but they only ever worked in silverplate. To date no examples have been found of any of the above thimbles.

The following silver thimbles were made in Australia or overseas for the Australian market between 1900 and 1950.

Aronson & Co.

Aronson & Co. of 297-299 Little Collins Street, Melbourne, were manufacturing jewellers and importers operating between 1902–1930, with branches in Brisbane, Adelaide and Sydney. The founder of the firm was Saul P. Aronson who had previously been in business with David Rosenthal in Melbourne from 1876 as Rosenthal, Aronson and Company.

Saul P. Aronson, head of Aronson and Company. 1912 (Australian Manufacturing Jewellers Watchmakers and Opticians Gazette August 1912)

Aronson & Co. were prolific advertisers to the retail trade, with their advertisements prominently placed at the beginning or even on the front covers of both the *Commonwealth Jeweller and Watchmaker* in Sydney and *Australian Manufacturing Jewellers, Watchmakers and Opticians Gazette* in Melbourne. Very few manufacturing jewellers at the time carried consistently prominent advertise-ments in both periodicals. From the inception of both periodicals, Aronson & Co. were the leading advertisers; from their advertisements we can gauge the range of merchandise and the company's importance.

According to an advertisement in *Australian Manufacturing Jewellers, Watchmakers and Opticians Gazette* in September 1919, Aronsons produced silver thimbles in three designs. This being just after the end of World War I, the advertisement runs: 'Owing to the uncertainty of getting Goods from England, we have decided to manufacture all lines previously imported...the Sterling Silver Thimbles are also made under the same secret process. Every Thimble is heavily strengthened with silver so that they are undentable, and they are made mostly in large sizes.' The thimbles would have been made for a very short period as the advertisements only ran for six months. Moreover, as the advertisements only appeared in the Melbourne based periodical, it is likely the thimbles were manufactured in Melbourne.

Only one example has been located of Aronson & Co.'s silver thimbles, corresponding to the middle thimble in the advertisement. This thimble has an all-over pattern of petalled daisies that flows on over the apex. Below that there is a band of three rows of waffle pattern and then a smaller, plain band and a rolled rim. Handling this thimble gives one the feeling of the skill of the thimblemaker; it is a thimble produced for sewing as well as being beautifully made.

The maker's marks are stamped with 'St S' for sterling silver in one rectangular lozenge, and 'A Co' in another lozenge. According to the list of Victorian jewellers who used the hallmarking system, Aronson's marks were 'A & Co' and a flag as their maker's mark. The thimbles existing from this period do not have the maker's mark and the & has been dropped. It is not known why Aronsons changed

SILVER THIMBLES

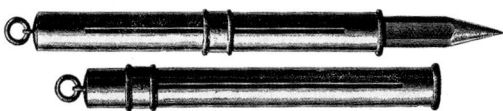

[Advertisement reproduction:]

24 The Australian Manufg. Jewellers', Watchmakers' and Opticians' Gazette. Sept., 1919

ARONSON & CO. PTY. LTD. London. Melbourne. 'Phone 159. Sydney. Brisbane. Adelaide.

THE
Very Latest Productions

Owing to the uncertainty of getting Goods from England, we have decided to
Manufacture all Lines Previously Imported.

9ct. Silver=lined Pencils

These Pencils are all Lined with Silver so that it is impossible to **DENT** them; they are made under the same Secret Process as our **well-known Undentable Bangles**

Sterling Silver Thimbles

The Sterling Silver Thimbles are also made under the same Secret Process. Every Thimble is Heavily Strengthened with Silver so that they are **Undentable**, and they are made mostly in Large Sizes.

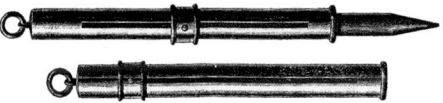

The least among our New Manufactures are PENCILS and THIMBLES, the scarcity of which in this Market demands immediate attention.
Watch Our Advertisements for Further Developments.

Aronson & Co of Melbourne silver thimble c.1919

First advertisement showing Aronson silver thimbles

the marks stamped on their thimbles when they had registered the trademark of a flag in 1903.

These thimbles by Aronsons pre-date the manufacture of Nifty and Elfin thimbles.

"AUSSIE"

When the first "AUSSIE" thimble was found, it was thought to have been a one-off made for a homesick Australian. The appearance of others, all found in Australia, negates this idea. In the Spring 1991 issue of *Thimble Notes and Queries* Wendy Ritchie, responding to the article by Iris Woolley on Australian thimbles, 'notes that another "AUSSIE" thimble has been found in Australia, so that there are three known examples in all'. The total is now five.

"AUSSIE" appears in bold upper case letters around the plain narrow band between inverted commas. On the verso, in four lozenges, is lettered St S (for sterling silver), a flag or anvil (the maker's mark) and 'S' 'L' (for steel-lined). The scrolled acanthus leaf pattern above the "AUSSIE" band has a cartouche in the design. On the rim there is a ribbed or patterned finish and the remaining part is well indented. There is variation in the scrolled pattern on all the "AUSSIE" thimbles found. There are no size marks but all examples seem to be the same size.

The "AUSSIE" thimbles are the only fully steel lined silver thimbles made in Australia and are similar in composition to Charles Horner's Dorcas thimbles. A magnet attracts the "AUSSIE".

The maker is still unknown and the mark could be either a flag or an anvil. As we have seen, Aronson & Co. did not use their known maker's mark of a flag on their silver thimbles so why would it be used on "AUSSIE" thimbles? The "AUSSIE" is also different in composition from the known examples of Aronson silver thimbles. The anvil was the mark of two other Australian jewellers. According to Cavill (1992), the anvil was the mark of W.F. Cole, a manufacturing jeweller in Brisbane between 1901 and 1988, who used the anvil mark between 1916–1945. A. Hiddlestone and Co. of Melbourne used the anvil mark from 1914 to 1927. They were bangle specialists. Any of these three could be the manufacturer of the "AUSSIE" with its flag or anvil mark, or none of them.

August Ludwig Brunkhorst

August Brunkhorst was born in Germany in 1846. He migrated to South Australia and settled in Adelaide in 1875 where he worked as a jeweller. According to Cavill (1992), 'it is highly probable that he was the "and Co" of Kindermann and Co., listed in Rundle Street, Adelaide during the period 1875–76'. Brunkhorst joined Kindermann in 1877. In 1883 he moved to join Henry J. Steiner, another German jeweller in the city. Steiner sold his business and remaining stock to Brunkhorst when he returned to live in Germany in 1884. Brunkhorst operated his firm as a jeweller in Adelaide until his death in 1919, when his business was purchased by Caris Bros of Western Australia.

The only silver thimble known to have survived with Brunkhorst's maker's marks reflects the style typical of his work, that Cavill (1992) describes as of 'relatively plain designs, free of excessive ornamentation, [which] were considered to be

LEFT *"AUSSIE" thimble from the front*
RIGHT *"AUSSIE" thimble from the verso, showing the marks for this steel-lined silver thimble*

August Brunkhorst's jewellery premises, corner Rundle and Charles Street Adelaide 1915 (Reproduced courtesy John Hawkins)

BRUNKHORST ADELAIDE

Brunkhorst of Adelaide, c.1890

more advanced than those of many of his contemporaries'. It is a plain elegant thimble, with a very defined rolled rim, and only the apex is indented. On this one known thimble, the monogram 'H E' in elegant Gothic script is the only adornment. The maker's marks are clearly stamped well inside the thimble in four separate lozenges. These read 'Brunkhorst Adelaide', with Brunkhorst's two other marks, a lion and a crown, still clearly visible alongside his name.

Comparing the marks on this lone thimble by Brunkhorst with the illustrations in Hawkins' (1973) table of Brunkhorst's marks, it is possible to date the thimble to *c.*1890.

Delarue & Co.

In 1850 Hippolyte F. Delarue founded his jewellery business in Sydney, trading as H.F. Delarue & Co. Delarue died in June 1881. From 1904 to 1925 the firm known as Delarue Ltd operated as watchmakers and jewellers at 378 George Street, Sydney.

Several silver thimbles exist with 'Delarue & Co Limd', and '378 George Street' underneath, pressed into the plain wide band. Some of these thimbles

Delarue & Co. of Sydney

have English hallmarks with the maker's marks of 'H.W Ltd' for Henry Williamson and the Chester hallmarks for 1904. The firm of Henry Williamson, London based, was in business as wholesalers from 1865 until 1931. The thimbles would not have been made by Henry Williamson, rather made for him by one of the big four silver thimble manufacturers who placed the wholesaler's initials on the band instead of their own. One can only speculate whether the Delarue advertising marks were added in Australia or England.

Another similar example of the Delarue thimbles exists, with the English marks of 'JF' for James Fenton and the Birmingham hallmarks for 1903. All the Delarue thimbles are tall, with a highly domed apex, and are indented all over with a plain wide band. It is possible that Fenton made the thimbles for Henry Williamson now that similar Fenton thimbles have been found for Delarue.

It was traditional in England at the time for jewellers to give these sorts of thimbles away with the purchase of a wedding ring. Delarue may have done the same.

Elfin

Although the Elfin silver thimbles are quite common in Australia, information on them is scarce. There are no maker's marks and no accompanying thimble boxes to identify the thimbles as Australian but they are still likely to be Australian made. An exhaustive search of the two periodicals for the manufacturing jewellery trade from 1910 to 1970 has turned up no evidence of the manufacturer of the Elfin thimble. In von Hoelle (1986), the Elfin is incorrectly ascribed to Price & Jardine of Sydney, who only made Nifty thimbles.

The first illustration of the Elfin thimble was traced to the July 1947 issue of *Commonwealth Jeweller and Watchmaker*. This periodical appeared monthly from 1916 to 1988 and was the official journal to the retail jewellery trade in Australia. The advertisement is for Roy A. Humphery, a 'wholesale jeweller' and importer of 92 Pitt Street, Sydney. A similar advertisement appeared in November 1947 and this second one appeared every month until July 1948. The advertisements show the thimble that we now recognise as the Elfin, with no mention of the thimble by name.

ROY A. HUMPHERY
Wholesale Jeweller and Importer
92 PITT STREET, SYDNEY

FOR IMMEDIATE DELIVERY ASSORTED SIZES

ONCE MORE AVAILABLE AFTER A LONG ABSENCE

STERLING SILVER THIMBLES
WITH STEEL REINFORCED ENDS

'Phone: BW8429 ——————— Your Orders

July 10, 1947.   The Commonwealth Jeweller and Watchmaker.   Page Ninety-three

First advertisement of Elfin thimble

Instead, the ad reads: 'Once more available after a long absence . . . for immediate delivery assorted sizes'. Comparing the photographs of Elfin thimbles with the advertisements from 1947 there is no doubt they are the same thimbles. A search of earlier advertisements (during and pre World War II) does not reveal any by Roy A. Humphery until June 1946. Why then 'after a long absence'? One can only speculate why no mention was made of the thimbles by their name of Elfin, and why there was no reference to the manufacturer. Advertisements with illustrations of the Elfin thimble continued into the 1950s—in these ads the thimbles that we now know as the Elfin were one of Roy A. Humphery's 'exclusive' lines. Could Humphery be the manufacturer of the Elfin? Being a wholesale jeweller, he may well have been, but there is nothing to link him as the manufacturer from these or any other advertisements.

From the advertisement we can see that Humphery was also an importer and one can speculate that the Elfin thimbles could have been imported. So far they have never been linked to any other country and it is more than likely that Humphery was acting as a wholesaler in their sale.

More important information follows in this advertisement: 'sterling silver thimbles with steel reinforced ends'. Having steel reinforced ends would make the Elfin a unique silver thimble worldwide. The Elfin thimbles are marked for sterling silver and thus one would not have contemplated testing them with a magnet for the presence of steel. Sadly this advertising is misleading as the Elfin thimbles do not attract a magnet, as they would if steel were present!

The Elfin's design has five to six rows of stylised half daisies or 'emu footprints'. This latter description first appeared in Woolley (1989) and was used again by Holmes in *Thimble Notes and Queries* (winter 1990). These daisy/prints are separated from the plain wide band by two grooves and there is no rolled rim. The centre of each daisy is

Elfin showing typical 'emu-print' daisy pattern

off centre to the row above. Poorly struck Elfin thimbles have the daisy/print pattern 'slipping down' into the grooves. The apex is indented. Elfins are all of the same design.

Holmes, in his *History of thimbles*, mistakenly mentions the Elfin as 'Elgin' in the paragraph on thimbles from Commonwealth countries. He suggests that these thimbles were made in imitation of English designs. This is not borne out with the Elfin design; it is peculiar to these Australian thimbles.

'Elfin' is stamped onto the wide band and 'Stg. Sil' in a lozenge on the verso. Elfins have only been found in five sizes, 2 to 6, with 6 being the smallest size. Size 2 is most commonly found. The size mark is pressed into the band, generally above the word 'Elfin'. Some Elfin thimbles have the size mark on the verso above 'Stg Sil and occasionally it appears on the side between 'Elfin' and 'Stg Sil'. On a few of these thimbles, the word 'Elfin' was poorly struck, and it would appear to read 'Elein'.

From the advertisements previously mentioned and the existence of Elfin thimbles with engravings for a wedding anniversary ('Mum and Dad 1948') and a birthday ('To Daphne with love Grandma 1949') on the bands, one can assume the Elfin thimbles were only made during the 1940s.

The trade mark for Elfin has never been registered in Australia for a thimble. Around forty Elfin thimbles exist in collections in Australia and nowhere else. Until proof of its manufacture is uncovered, we must presume the Elfin thimbles to be Australian.

Fairfax & Roberts

Fairfax & Roberts of 23–25 Hunter Street in Sydney have been jewellers and watchmakers since 1883. Between the years of 1899 and 1903, Fairfax & Roberts imported silver James Fenton thimbles from in England. These thimbles have a highly domed apex and are indented all over, with a plain band. They all bear the Birmingham hallmark and date letters of 1899 to 1903. On the band the words 'Fairfax & Roberts Sydney' are stamped (the word 'Sydney' is underneath the jeweller's name, bounded by a line on each side). The quality of the lettering is not good and with use has largely worn off. The English hallmarks are, on the other hand, still clearly legible. Several examples of these thimbles still exist.

Elfin thimbles showing the three various positions of the size numbers. The most commonly found appears second from the left

LEFT *Elfin poorly struck showing 'Elein'*
RIGHT *Elfin thimble showing an engraved date*

Fairfax & Roberts were and still are one of Sydney's leading jewellers. These thimbles were given away with the purchase of a wedding ring.

It is interesting to find two Sydney jewellers, Delarue and Fairfax & Roberts, using very similar English hallmarked silver thimbles with their firm's name engraved onto the band: Delarue included the street name, Fairfax & Roberts the city name, over the same time span. The period of manufacture of these thimbles was no more than five years,

Fairfax & Roberts, Sydney jewellers

between 1899 and 1904, according to the English hallmarks.

James Fenton

James Fenton, which manufactured thimbles in Birmingham between 1839 and 1930, was one of the big four English silver thimble manufacturers. It is rare to find examples of Fenton sterling silver thimbles with an Australian connection but three do exist.

Fairfax & Roberts and Delarue & Co. are two examples of Australian jewellers using James Fenton silver thimbles to promote the sale of wedding rings to their Sydney clients at the turn of the century.

There is one known example of a James Fenton silver thimble with an Australian place name on the band. This in itself is rare: Fenton did not make many thimbles with place names on. The example found has 'Queensland' in ornate lettering embossed around the band and bears a Birmingham 1908 hallmark. The waffle pattern on the top half of the thimble is separated from the band by two grooves. The band is separated from the rolled rim by another pair of fine grooves.

The lettering on Fenton place-name thimbles is not as crisp as those made by Henry Griffith and Sons who were the major place-name thimble manufacturers. The lettering for 'Queensland' is different from the place-name thimbles made by both Griffith and James Fenton, whose other thimbles have the place name in high relief. The embossing is an integral part of the thimble and would not have been added to the thimble in Australia. It is a unique thimble and one wonders whether thimbles were made by Fenton for other Australian states. None have been noted for Henry Griffith.

James Fenton's Queensland thimble

Gabler Brothers

Although they were a German firm of thimble manufacturers, Gabler made enamel thimbles for the Australian souvenir market. Gabler Bros was formed in Schorndorf in southern Germany in 1850, when Gabler's sons took over the thimble making business their father had started in 1824. In the 1920s and 1930s Gabler Bros made enamel and silver thimbles for tourist outlets around the world. These included St Peters in Rome, the Cathedral in Florence and the Ponte Vecchio in Florence. Egyptian scenes and Dutch windmill scenes in blue enamel also appear in the Gabler catalogues. Gabler Bros continued making thimbles until 1963.

According to the catalogue of Gabler thimbles edited by Jungbludt (1988), Gabler Bros had between seven and eight million thimbles in stock at any one time. This would have made them the largest thimble factory in the world. Jungbludt notes: 'Particular sensitivity was required in the handling of the export market, in particular in adapting to the different tastes of the individual countries.' This catalogue only illustrates 1700 thimbles, but Gabler's pattern books contained over 4000 designs. From these pattern books the Australian thimble design would have been chosen.

These Gabler thimbles portray the Sydney Harbour Bridge and were first mentioned and photographed in Lundquist's *Book of a thousand thimbles* (1970). On meeting Myrtle Lundquist in Pasadena at a thimble conference in 1980, Iris Woolley asked her about this thimble as Iris felt it belonged in Australia. Myrtle's response was, 'You have the bridge in Sydney, I only have the thimble.'

The bridge across Sydney Harbour was opened on 19 March 1932. Gabler Bros produced these silver thimbles with brightly coloured scenic enamel bands, showing the Harbour Bridge, with the Sydney coat of arms on the verso. Luna Park, a fun fair, is included in the scene. The Park opened in October 1935 so these thimbles could not have been produced to commemorate the opening of the Bridge three years earlier. Being made in the 1930s the enamel band would not have been handpainted, rather the design would be a transfer or decal under the enamel.

The word 'Sydney' is lettered on the side of the enamel band. The thimbles have an attractively scrolled rolled rim and the area above the enamel band is indented, including the apex. The word 'Sterling' in a lozenge is stamped into second row of the indentations above the enamel band. In Zalkin (1988), in describing German enamel thimbles mention is made of stamping the silver mark in the second row of the indentations as the clue to the country of origin. According to Frank (1993), German thimbles made for export had the word 'Sterling' stamped into the indentations instead of the usual .800 mark. Both references go on to link these early German enamels with Gabler.

An eight-pointed star is on the apex. Gabler registered this trademark but never patented it, which meant that other German thimble makers have copied it.

These Sydney Harbour Bridge enamel thimbles would have been made by Gabler and not by another German thimble manufacturer of the time. The design is similar to other examples of Gabler's work dating from the twenties and thirties. According to Frank (1993), most of the Gabler enamelled thimbles had the enamelling around the bottom half of the thimble, as do these Sydney Harbour Bridge thimbles. They are of excellent quality and an important early thimble design made overseas for the Australian market.

Boxes for the Sydney Harbour Bridge thimble are still in existence but they bear no maker's marks. They are a deep red shade and the thimbles are seated on a wooden post in the thimble cases (Plate 1).

Gabler's Sydney Harbour Bridge enamel on silver

Henry Griffith and Sons

The firm of Henry Griffith and Sons of Leamington Spa was one of the big four silver thimble manufacturers in England at the turn of the century. They were the makers of the Empire thimbles, significant to Australia.

The Empire sterling silver thimble first came to attention in the winter 1989 issue of the *Thimble Society of London* where it was described as unrecorded at the time. It was for sale as the 'Commonwealth thimble', although the Commonwealth of Nations only came into being in 1926.

Registration numbers on thimbles are stamped with the letters R^D followed by a number. Registration with the Public Records Office (in England) after 1883 protected the design of a thimble so that it could not be copied for five years. The Empire thimbles carry the registered design number R^D 356898, which was issued in May 1900 to Frederick Griffith, one of Henry Griffith's sons. Although there was such keen competition between the recognised thimble manufacturers that most designs were copied as soon as they were out of the registration period, this design has never been copied by any other thimble manufacturer.

It is not known what term Griffith used for this design but they are known by thimble collectors as 'Empire thimbles', so-called because they have a distinct border of seven emblems representing countries of the British Empire at the turn of this century. The emblems, each with their place lettered underneath, reading to the right from the England emblem (a lion over a large crown), are: Australia (an upright kangaroo), Canada (a beaver on a log), New Zealand (four stars—the Southern Cross), Tasmania (a lion rampant), India (an elephant), Natal (two wildebeest).

Two versions exist for Canada, the beaver on the log and a maple leaf. This minor change would not have necessitated a change to the registration number. It seems strange, however, that Griffith included two emblems for Australia. Why was the lion chosen to represent Tasmania? Tasmania's coat of arms has a lion as part of the design, but this only came into being in 1917. Also, why did Griffith represent only Natal on the Empire thimbles when both Natal and the Cape of Good Hope were British states in South Africa at the turn of the century?

Above the border of emblems are two rows of well-indented large-petalled daisies, with the daisies continuing over the apex.

The marks on the band of the Empire thimbles are: R^D 356898 stamped on the band; the size (all known examples are size 15); the hallmarks for Chester of 1899, 1900 and 1901 (remember that

Chester changed its date letter every July, so two of these thimbles could have been made in the same year of 1900). The thimblemaker's marks of 'HG Ltd' in a lozenge are for Henry Griffith, although not the usual marks of 'H G & S' that Griffith used at the turn of the century. Some examples of the Empire thimble also exist with marks for 'A B & Co.' instead of 'HG Ltd'. These are the marks for A. Bromet & Co., who were wholesale jewellers in London. According to Holmes in *Thimble Notes and Queries* (autumn 1991), Charles Horner made thimbles for Bromet. The marks of 'A. B & Co.' on the Empire thimbles indicate that Griffith also made thimbles for Bromet. Abraham Bromet traded as wholesale jewellers from 1878 to 1890 but the business was only wound up in 1910.

On one example of the Empire thimbles in Australia the current maker's mark of 'HG Ltd' has clearly been superimposed over an earlier mark. (see below)

Queen Victoria died in January 1901, several months after the design Empire was registered. The Thimble Society of London speculated in 1989 whether the thimble that they were offering for sale with a 1901 hallmark had been made to commemorate the coronation of Edward VII (this was to have taken place in 1901, but owing to illness, he was not crowned until 1902). Now that thimbles have been located with earlier Chester hallmarks this theory seems invalid. If these were commemorative thimbles, what were they commemorating? Holmes in his *Thimble Notes and Queries* (summer 1990) suggests that all these emblems 'merely reflected the popular enthusiasm for the British Empire that was ruling at the time'. Without any other evidence to the contrary, Holmes' theory may be correct.

The Empire thimble is one of the significant English thimbles of the late nineteenth and early twentieth centuries and is a beautiful example of Victorian silversmithing—it warrants a couple of views showing off the two Australian emblems.

Other Henry Griffith and Sons silver thimbles with a more tenuous connection with Australia exist. These thimbles were made for the P & O

LEFT *Henry Griffith's Empire thimble, showing the Tasmania emblem*
RIGHT *Empire thimble with the Australia emblem*

Shipping Line whose ships plied between England and Australia in the first half of this century. P & O liners which had thimbles produced for them include the *Orion, Orantes, Orsova* and *Orcades*. These thimbles began to be made shortly after World War II, production ceasing in 1956 when Henry Griffith stopped making thimbles. The *Orion* operated between 1935 and 1963.

The P & O thimbles have closely-knit daisies with huge centres on the apex and upper half. The band is finely ribbed with the lettering for the ship's name in relief. The size and the maker's marks, 'HG & S' in a lozenge, and Birmingham hallmarks, are punched on the rim.

Henry Griffith's P & O Orion thimble

L. Orbuck

The only reference found to Australian silver Christmas pudding charms is in an advertisement in the November 1922 issue of *Commonwealth Jeweller and Watchmaker*, where L. Orbuck of 288 Little Collins Street Melbourne advertised 'Xmas Pudding sets: ring, thimble, wishbone and button 4 pieces complete on card. Made in Australia in Sterling Silver . . .'. In later ads in *Australian Manufacturing Jeweller*, although Christmas pudding sets were advertised, the charms were not specified. It would be wonderful to be able to identify

SILVER THIMBLES

> **XMAS**
> Ring, Thimble, Wishbone, Button.
> **PUDDING SETS**
> 4 pieces complete on card.
> Made in Australia in Sterling Silver
> Insist on having Australian made.
> If your wholesaler has none write to
> **L. ORBUCK**
> 288 Little Collins Street, Melbourne.

Rare advertisement for thimble pudding charms 1922 (Commonwealth Jeweller and Watchmaker November 1922)

today the miniature thimbles made by Orbuck more than 70 years ago.

Pall Mall EPNS

During the 1920s and 1930s thousands of souvenir thimbles were made in Europe for distribution to tourist outlets around the world. This included Australia. The 1930s souvenir thimbles show the Sydney Harbour Bridge on an affixed enamel badge. As part of the badge there is a castle shape above the badge. As with the Gabler Sydney Harbour Bridge thimbles, these thimbles include Luna Park in the design, so the thimbles must postdate 1935, not 1932 when the Bridge was first opened (*Plate 2*).

The thimbles are stamped with 'Pall Mall EPNS 8 [the size] Germany' on the rim opposite to the badge. The body of the thimbles is plainly indented. These early tourist thimbles differ from those made today where the badge, wrapped around the thimble, is a more integral part of the thimble.

PALL MALL EPNS 8 Germany

Price & Jardine

The Nifty thimbles, made by Price & Jardine of Sydney, are the best known Australian silver thimbles today. From humble beginnings in 1916 the firm of Price & Jardine grew to be the largest manufacturing jewellers in New South Wales.

Ernest Hawthorne (Ernie) Price started as a jeweller with Crown Jewellery Co. in George Street, Sydney. He then became head of Price & Co., a retail jewellery firm, in King Street, Sydney. In 1916 Price joined H.C. Jardine to form Price & Jardine Ltd, manufacturing jewellers. In 1939 he withdrew from participation in Price & Jardine, but the firm retained the name until it ceased trading in 1971. Price then linked his interests with those of his son in the firm of E.H. Price & Co., stock and station agents. Ernie Price died in February 1948.

Henry Charles Jardine served his apprenticeship as a jeweller in Sydney with E.J. Coote and at Messrs Morris & Wigny. In August 1904 Jardine entered into partnership with W. Grant to form Grant & Jardine at 136 Pitt Street Sydney. After only three years the firm was thoroughly established and they moved to larger and larger premises, ending up in 516 Kent Street. At about that time Grant severed his connection with the firm. The partnership begun in Kent Street with Ernie Price in 1916, in a limited liability company, saw the foundation of one of Sydney's most successful jewellery firms, known as Price & Jardine. From the beginnings in 1905 when there was one employee, the staff grew to 100 by 1942. In 1922 Price & Jardine built their own large modern factory at 431 Elizabeth Street in Sydney, which was to be their premises until they ceased trading. This original 1922 building still stands. H.C. Jardine was a member of the Goldsmiths and Silversmiths' Association of New South Wales. He died in April 1945 at the age of 65.

Mr Jack Jardine, brother of the founder, was also associated with the firm.

Mr H.C. Jardine's son Walter (known as Jim), joined the firm in 1928. He played an active role as a Company Director in charge of the Tool and Die Sinking Department until the company was sold in 1971.

The first advertisement for Price and Jardine Ltd appeared in *Commonwealth Jeweller and Watchmaker* in July 1918. They were listed as 'manufacturers of

Private Jack Jardine, brother of the co-founder of Price & Jardine 1918 (Commonwealth Jeweller and Watchmaker April 1918)

all classes of jewellery' in Sydney in the Fairlight Buildings at 516 Kent Street.

In August 1922, the first mention of the name Nifty appeared in an advertisement in *Commonwealth Jeweller and Watchmaker*. It was for the 'Nifty hairpin, mounted in 9ct. gold'. The ads claimed that these early Nifty products all had their designs registered but no records of this could be traced. It is interesting that the firm's name did not always appear in these and subsequent advertisements. Price & Jardine and Nifty Products seem to be synonymous from 1933 onwards, as by then they were well known for their Nifty jewellery.

In an article about Price & Jardine in April 1933, the first reference to the Nifty thimble appeared:

'... will be producing a silver steel-lined thimble at a much lower price than the famous imported article.' One must deduce that it was the Dorcas thimble that was being referred to. The Nifty was never made as a silver steel-lined thimble, however.

In the following month, May 1933, Price & Jardine first offered Nifty thimbles for sale to the trade. This advertisement appeared in *Commonwealth Jeweller and Watchmaker* and included the first mention of 'solid silver thimbles' amongst other Nifty products. Nifty thimbles did not appear in many of their advertisements, in fact it is rare to find them mentioned as they were a very small part of Price & Jardine's output. The last advertisement to carry mention of Nifty thimbles appeared in October 1939. For examples of these Nifty thimble advertisements see Appendix 5.

The photograph that appeared in *Commonwealth Jeweller and Watchmaker* in August 1935 shows some of the Price & Jardine staff engaged in production work—most of these staff were long-term employees. The interview which accompanied the photographs and illustrations of the new up-to-date machinery made mention that the new machines were the only ones of their kind in New South Wales.

JULY 1st, 1918.   THE COMMONWEALTH JEWELLER AND WATCHMAKER.   39

Price & Jardine Ltd.

Manufacturing Jewellers

SYDNEY

Manufacturers of all classes of Jewellery

Sole Proprietors of Wax Proof Box Snap Bangles

Fairlight Buildings   Telephone: CITY 34   516 Kent Street

First advertisement for Price & Jardine

RIGHT *First use of trade name Nifty* (Commonwealth Jeweller and Watchmaker *August 1922*)

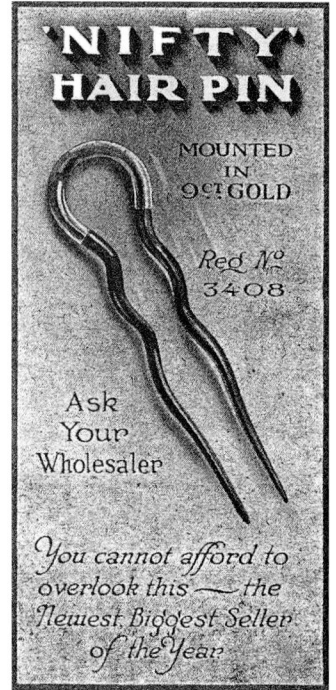

*Price & Jardine's first Nifty thimble advertisement (*Commonwealth Jeweller and Watchmaker *May 1933)*

RIGHT *Photo 1 shows Messrs E.H. Price with W.J. Jardine bending; photo 2 shows Ernie Blunt, Vic Clarkson and Sid Brown, a metallurgist, with Jack Jardine on his own in the third photo (*Commonwealth Jeweller and Watchmaker *August 1935)*

From May 1933 onwards Price & Jardine placed an advertisement in *Commonwealth Jeweller and Watchmaker*—usually a full page—every month until the late 1950s, when their advertisements appeared only sporadically. From this lengthy sequence we can trace the development of new, wide ranging products from this firm of manufacturing jewellers, whose advertisements were as varied as they were many. Their products are a social commentary on what the people of Australia were buying in the thirties. By placing a different advertisement every month until the outbreak of World War II, Price & Jardine helped to shape the idea of their firm as keen, practical, quality jewellers. Whilst hundreds of Price & Jardine and Nifty advertisements were published over a thirty-year period, only four types of advertisements mentioned silver Nifty thimbles. A list of products manufactured by Price & Jardine may be found in Appendix 5, as well as the remaining thimble advertisements.

They were successful as manufacturing jewellers because they realised they had to enter into competition with imported goods. That they were local, reliable, and ready to support their guarantees of quality, and that their goods were made in Australia, by Australians, ensured the success of their enterprise. Their lines were sold throughout Australia and New Zealand. The regular articles on Price & Jardine which appeared in *Commonwealth Jeweller and Watchmaker* make absorbing reading, with a picture emerging of a solid innovative firm of jewellers keeping abreast of trends as fashion dictated.

Price & Jardine manufactured articles in 9 carat gold, 9 carat silver-lined, silver, chromium plate and stainless steel. All bore the trademark Nifty, were made in Australia and supplied through the wholesale and retail trade.

The firm suspended manufacture of their Nifty products during World War II when Japan entered the war and from August 1942 they became aircraft parts and war materials manufacturers. Throughout the war years Price & Jardine advertisements continued in *Commonwealth Jeweller and Watchmaker* every month, carrying a message of this war work.

When the factory was again ready for jewellery production after the war, whilst their advertisements continued, thimbles never appeared in them again. From this it is certain that thimbles were no longer being made. It is no wonder there are so few Nifty thimbles still in existence today when they were only produced over an 8 to 10 year period between 1933–1942.

Mr Price was one of the leading proponents for the use of the proposed hallmarking system under discussion for New South Wales in the 1920s. 'P.J.P.' was the registered mark for Price & Jardine, but no silver thimbles with this mark have survived, if they were made.

It is interesting to speculate on the name 'Nifty'. Why was it chosen? According to Mrs Peggy Jardine, widow of Jim Jardine, her father-in-law chose the word to encapsulate the type of jewellery he was creating and the image he wanted to project.

An application for the Nifty trademark was registered on 6 January 1947 by Price & Jardine Pty Limited, 431 Elizabeth Street, Sydney. The Registration number is 89,829 and is for jewellery, imitation jewellery and metal attachments for watches. It seems strange to only register the Nifty name twenty-five years after it was first used, but this is the only registration of the Nifty name in Australia by Price & Jardine.

A delightful story comes from a woman who joined Price & Jardine in 1935 at the age of 15. When she applied to them for employment, she was asked whether she could use a machine. Thinking they meant a sewing machine, she said yes. She was horrified to find that she was expected to use a stamping machine in their press department! She soon learnt the technique and for the next five years she was responsible for putting the daisies on the Nifty thimbles. Price & Jardine employed a large proportion of women.

Holmes (1985) has a photograph of the Nifty thimble alongside an English silver thimble to illustrate his point that 'taking advantage of protective tariffs, several silversmiths in Australia sought to emulate the established thimble manufacturers in Britain by making branded thimbles of their own ... but the quality was not as good as that of the imported article'. The English thimble's daisies seem more firmly punched into the metal, confirming Holmes' comment.

From observation, all Nifty thimbles have an identical design: three rows of large daisies and a

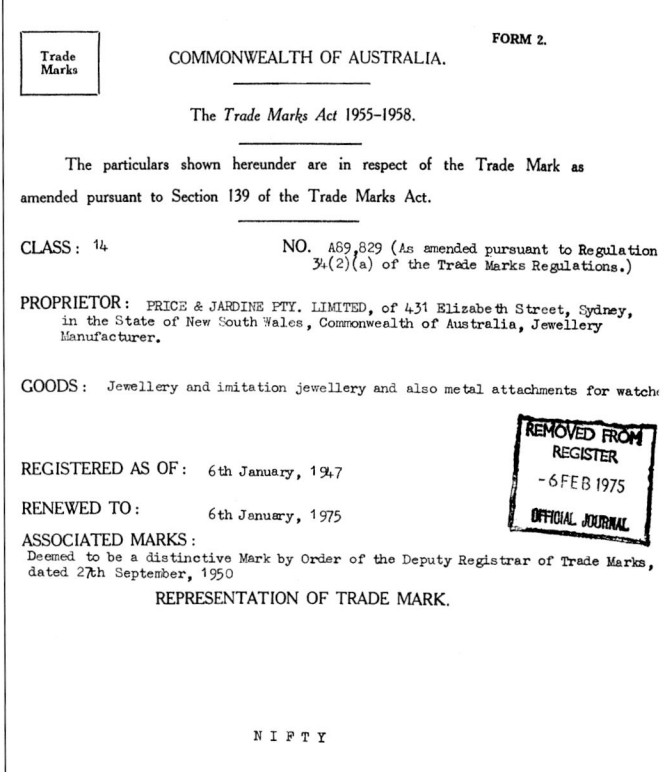

The only trade mark registration for Nifty

wide band, separated by two fine bands of Xs. On some existing thimbles, the centre of the daisy is very deeply defined and some have X patterns more ornate than others. The centres of the daisies are not centred one above the other on the majority of Nifty thimbles. Rarely one finds the centres of the daisies lined up, which gives the impression the thimbles are faceted. This is not so, it is just the effect of the daisies being in vertical lines, with the centres lined up. The daisy pattern is carried over the apex and on mint condition Nifty thimbles one can observe a fine scalloped edge to the apex. The variations are minor and indicate that quality control was not as tight then as we have come to expect today.

"Nifty'. Stg. Silver.' is stamped on the thimble band. Size marks appear on the band after 'Silver'.

As with the Elfin thimbles, five sizes of Niftys are found, ranging from 6 to 10; 10 is the smallest while 8 is the most common size to have survived.

Nothing on the thimbles identifies them with Australia. They were, however, supplied in cardboard thimble boxes from which the Nifty can be identified as Australian made. The words 'Sterling Silver "Nifty" Made in Australia' appear on the outside of the boxes, but there is no mention of Price & Jardine. The boxes are dark maroon with gold lettering, lined with dark blue velvet.

Nifty thimble with its original box

LEFT *Nifty sterling silver made by Price & Jardine of Sydney*
RIGHT *Rarer Nifty with daisies in vertical lines*

LEFT *Nifty with daisy centres well defined and the 'pie crust' edge on the apex*
RIGHT *Nifty apexes, also showing variations in the daisy pattern*

H.H. Halls & Co. were distributing agents briefly for Nifty products in 1924 but no thimbles were mentioned in their advertisements. Bloch & Gerber Ltd of 46 York Street, Sydney, was one of the wholesale houses that supplied Nifty merchandise to the retail jewellery trade. Their advertisements appeared regularly in *Commonwealth Jeweller and Watchmaker* after World War II but Nifty thimbles never appeared in these advertisements either. Milne Browne & Co. Ltd of Sydney were also agents for Nifty products during 1951 but again no thimbles were mentioned in their advertisements. Roy A. Humphery, a wholesale jeweller and importer at 92 King Street, Sydney, also advertised Nifty products for sale but again no Nifty thimbles are mentioned in his ads in *Commonwealth Jeweller and Watchmaker* in the late 1940s.

Walter Jardine's sons did not enter the firm and Price & Jardine ceased trading in March 1971 when the firm was sold to Ranleigh Ware of Adelaide. Ranleigh had been specialists in the manufacture of stainless trays since 1927.

As part of the biennial Thimble Collectors International (TCI) Conventions, held in the

United States, there is an auction of thimbles. At the 1988 Convention in Spokane two Australian thimbles were amongst the items auctioned. The Nifty fetched US$180 and the Elfin reached US$120. It is pleasing to note the high prices realised in this international thimble forum from international collectors, as there were collectors in Australia who felt that these thimbles should have remained in Australia.

1950—

No new manufacturers of silver thimbles have replaced the Nifty and Elfin manufacturers in Australia in the second half of the twentieth century. Individual silversmiths have created thimbles, some by hand, others by casting. As with earlier thimbles, there is no hallmarking system and one has had to rely on silversmiths and jewellers to use distinctive punchmarks. A good proportion of silversmiths is unfortunately content to only have the silver content marked on their silver thimbles with no maker's marks.

The most commonly used symbol guaranteeing the quality of sterling silver since 1950 is 925— differing from the earlier Australian thimble makers, who used the abbreviated words for sterling silver.

The following list cannot hope to be complete but it is compiled from the result of surveys amongst the formal thimble collecting community in Australia today.

Eric Car

Eric Car of Fremantle in Western Australia is a gold and silversmith who made silver thimbles in 1979. The thimbles are heavy in weight with handmade, widely spaced indentations all over. A fine zigzag band separates the indents from the band. There is also a second band of zigzag pattern at the rim which is rolled.

The band is stamped with the size mark and 'S St' in a lozenge with a [black] swan, also in a lozenge, as the maker's mark. The thimbles were sold with the maker's card.

Frank Cowan

Frank Cowan of South Australia made this attractive silver thimble. It was purchased in Hahndorf in South Australia in 1980, but there are no further details about Frank Cowan or other thimbles produced by him.

The all-over design—a stylised leaf pattern— also covers the apex. There is a rolled rim and the maker's marks are above the rim, stamped with 'Stg Sil' with a hopping kangaroo mark and the maker's mark 'FHC' in a lozenge and 'L' for the size, large.

Frank Cowan of Hahndorf

Bryan Fraser

Bryan Fraser of Artistry in Brass, Caringbah in New South Wales, was a maker of doll jewellery and accessories as well as doll house accessories. Fraser placed advertisements in the doll collectors' magazines advertising that he made sterling silver, mother-of-pearl, brass and copper thimbles as well as old fashioned finger protectors. He died in 1995. Unfortunately no examples of his silver thimbles could be traced.

Genesis

These modern silver thimbles, dating from the 1990s, are engraved all around the body of the thimble with an acanthus leaf design. The apex is stepped down from the lip of the thimble—a further protection for preventing the needle from

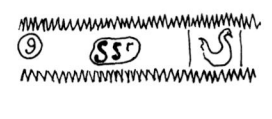

Eric Car of Fremantle

slipping off when sewing. There is a plain wide band and a rolled rim. The thimbles are marked 'Stg' and '.925' on the band. There are no maker's marks.

The thimbles are boxed and the word 'Genesis' is lettered on the inside lid of the thimble boxes. No other information is available.

Genesis silver

Georgina

Miniature silver thimbles were made by Georgina in Sydney in the 1990s. Being only 7 mm (¼") in height, there is no room for maker's marks, so the thimbles are accompanied by the maker's card bearing the words 'Georgina' 'Solid Sterling Silver' 'Made in Australia'. The thimbles are hand indented all over and there is a loop on the rim.

Georgina of Sydney's silver charm thimble

German silver

A recent addition to the range of modern silver thimbles available in Australia are enamel thimbles with a koala design. Though no maker's marks appear on the thimbles, the eight-pointed star used by most German silversmiths, after the Gabler star, is on the apex, indicating that the thimble is made in Germany. '925 M' is stamped up in the apex: the 'M' is for the size, medium. The rolled rim is plain.

White translucent enamel covering the whole body of the thimbles over guilloche gives the thimbles a delicate, almost three-dimensional, effect. There is a small scene of a koala in a tree on the front and 'Australia' is lettered diagonally across the verso (*Plate 3*).

Several modern silver thimblemakers in Germany today are continuing the tradition established by the Gabler Bros. This thimble design could be attributed to any one of them, though Julius Wengert of Pforzheim is the most likely, as they are similar to other enamelled thimbles made by him.

Peter Gertler

The Embroiderers Guild Victoria commissioned limited edition, sterling silver- and gold-dipped thimbles to commemorate their 30th birthday in 1990. The thimbles were designed and made by the silversmith Peter Gertler. The design incorporates the Guild emblem and the dates 1960–1990.

Adrian Graham-Rowe

Adrian Graham-Rowe, of Kalbar in Queensland, makes silver thimbles. Turning from his creative work of fleece-picture making, Adrian started silver making and produced silver buckles by hand. Not being a formally trained silversmith Adrian, has put much thought into his thimbles. He creates the thimbles by hand and then engraves the pattern onto them. His thimbles have a variety of brightcut patterns with hand punched indentations on the apex. Few, if any, other modern Australian thimble makers decorate their silver thimbles with brightcut engraving. There are no maker's marks on his thimbles.

Adrian has also created silver thimble cages to house his thimbles, so that they can be worn around the neck. His output has not been large, being a hobbyist. Adrian makes thimbles to size on commission.

Adrian Graham-Rowe of Laidley

Pat Hagan

Pat Hagan is a well known South Australian silversmith who has worked with precious metals since the early sixties. In the last twelve years Hagan has turned her hobby into a business. She makes thimbles for groups as well as by commission, in a range of sizes.

Pat's thimbles are dainty in shape. The body is unindented and smooth, with two grooves, and has an applied decoration. The apex has widely spaced indentations. Her designs with a Sturt's desert pea for South Australia are most distinctive. Other designs include the wombat, South Australia's fauna emblem, and koalas. These silver thimbles are often presented by the South Australian Governor to visiting VIPs. Thimbles are also made with Cowell jade tops. Pat's thimbles can be engraved and can have virtually any design—her versatility makes her range most appealing. Her latest concept is a silver thimble where the cap lifts off. The cap can be highly ornamented without detracting from the utility of the thimble.

Other than their distinctive shape, Hagan's thimbles have 'Sterling No. ..' stamped inside the rim to identify them.

Some of Hagan's thimbles are packaged in red gum or blackwood boxes, also made by her. The boxes are cylindrical in shape and if the apex of the thimble has a special decoration, its box has a hole in the lid so that the design can be seen. Gift presentations such as these only enhance the desirability of Pat's thimbles.

Pat Hagan approached the Embroiderers Guild of South Australia to design and make silver thimbles and membership brooches for their members. As they were commissioned to celebrate South Australia's Sesquicentenary in 1986 the thimbles have a Sturt's desert pea affixed to the body, which is otherwise completely plain; the apex is hand indented. 'Embroiderers Guild of South Australia' is lettered around the thimbles below two grooves.

The thimbles were launched at the Guild's Exhibition of Embroidery that ran from 1–16 March 1986. The Exhibition was opened on 28 February by the Patron of the Guild, Lady Dunstan, who was presented with thimble No.1. This was displayed in a special box with the top of the thimble forming part of the lid of the box. The rest of the thimbles are stamped 'Sterling No...' on the inside rim. This numbering is done for groups who commission thimbles. One hundred thimbles were commissioned by the Guild and they are still available. These were the only thimbles made for the South Australian Guild.

Pat has recently had her silver thimbles promoted by Sewmail, an Australian mail order service. The two designs available are an echidna or gumnuts, both in the style where the decoration is on a removable cap. The rest of the thimble is plain with only the apex indented. These thimbles are available in two sizes.

Pat Hagan's Embroiderers Guild of South Australia

Diana Hales

Diana Hales, from the Blue Mountains in New South Wales, crafted silver and brass jewellery, hair ornaments, bracelets and necklaces and thimbles, all with fine detail of Australian wildflowers and animals. Hales used no maker's mark. Only one example of her thimbles has been encountered. The thimble is not tapered, having very straight sides. It has a large gumnut on the apex, with a gum leaf falling from the apex down the side. The body of the thimble is smooth with a handpunched design.

Diana Hales of the Blue Mountains

Ian Hannay

Ian Hannay learned silversmithing at the Fremantle Tech in Western Australia and initially repaired jewellery for friends. He graduated into jewellery making. During 1993, Ian responded to the challenge by Gallery One and made a variety of silver thimbles. They are squat in shape, with slight striations on the body and crudely handpunched indentations on the apex. Hannay uses wildflowers

Pat Hagan of South Australia's wombat

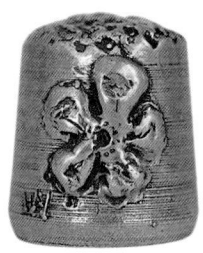

Ian Hannay of Perth

in relief as the decoration on his thimbles. These include Geraldton wax and some of Western Australia's everlasting daisies.

The thimbles are inscribed with a 'WAYV' conjoined mark on the outside rim, chosen to represent Yvonne Varey of Gallery One who commissioned them. Very few of these thimbles were ever made.

Louis Hermann

In 1993, the Embroiderers Guild of Queensland Inc. celebrated its 25th anniversary. The Guild commissioned a sterling silver thimble to commemorate its founding in 1968. Louis Hermann, an ornamental engraver originally from Hungary, designed the thimble. From his design the thimbles were cast in .925 silver by Les Hyde and the result is a delightful commemorative. The design has an all-over pattern which includes the apex, of Cooktown orchids, the state flower of Queensland. The plain band is engraved with 'Embroiderers' Guild Qld'. The thimbles are stamped '.925' either on the band or inside the rim. The maker's marks are illegible.

As the thimbles were designed to be used, there are four sizes available: S, M, L and XL. The sizes are not marked on the thimbles, which are supplied in a blue drawstring pouch with a descriptive leaflet.

More than 500 of these thimbles have been sold and they are still available from the Guild.

Louis Hermann's Embroiderers Guild of Queensland

Curtis Hine

Curtis Hine's main work is restoration and repair of antique and modern metal articles for the antique trade. He is a practising silversmith who, except for a 16-week course he attended in 1973 to learn basic silversmithing skills, is self taught. Since 1973 he has handcrafted a number of commission pieces such as jewellery (including a Bishop's cross), buttons, photo frames, spoons, boxes and trophy cups, all in sterling silver.

Hine, of Balwyn North in Melbourne, started making sterling silver thimbles in 1989, working from his home. His thimbles are all made by hand, not cast. They usually have smooth sides, are quite tall, and have an indented apex. Curtis makes a wide range of thimbles. He leaves some completely plain, embosses others with roses or geometric designs and some have Australian fauna (kangaroo, koala), boomerangs or Australian maps applied. The thimbles are stamped 'H.C.H. Stg. Sil' inside the rim.

Curtis Hine of Balwyn's engraved rose

According to Hine's records, he has made in excess of 200 silver thimbles, which makes him the most prolific silver thimble maker in Australia today. The thimbles are available in ten sizes, suitable for both adults and children. They are made for use as well as for the collectors' market.

Pat Holcombe

Pat Holcombe is a Brisbane silver and goldsmith, who makes jewellery. Pat started silversmithing as a hobby whilst living in Albuquerque, New Mexico, in 1979. She now works full time as a silversmith and enameller and produces high quality jewellery and trinkets, including spoons and silver pudding charms. She also makes silver thimbles and has done

Pat Holcombe of Brisbane

so since late 1988, handmaking two or three a year. Since exhibiting her silver thimbles at the annual Brookfield Show in Brisbane (where quilting forms 80% of the needlework section), the demand from quilters for Pat's thimbles has grown.

Her thimbles are available in two sizes and are made with two apexes—flat for a quilter's use and more domed for embroidery; both are hand indented. Being handmade the patterning differs from thimble to thimble—this makes each one individual. Some have pierced designs. Pat Holcombe can be commissioned to make thimbles.

Holcombe's thimbles have always been marked with her distinctive punchmark of a decorated boomerang forming her name, Pat, and the word 'Sterling' inside the thimbles.

Richard Ivey

Richard Ivey is a well known silversmith in Laura, South Australia, and his jewellery is sold as far away as Melbourne. Being a silversmith it was not difficult for Richard to make silver thimbles. His thimbles have a rounded apex which is hand indented. The sides are not indented, having a scrolled engraving as the design. The rim is rolled and the thimbles are stamped '.925' in a lozenge above the rim. The thimble illustrated was made in 1988. There are no maker's marks.

Richard Ivey of Laura

Daniel Jenkins

Daniel Jenkins, a silversmith from Maling Road in Melbourne, made sterling silver thimbles in 1983 with gumnuts and leaves around the band. Having seen his beautiful silver and brass tatting shuttles, Beryl Warne of Thimble Collections commissioned him to make these silver thimbles. They worked together on the design and style of the gumleaf thimbles.

The apex and main body of the thimbles have stippled indentations giving a good surface to grip the needle, which means the thimbles could be used for sewing. The decoration is a fine band of gumnuts and leaves on the rim. The thimbles were available with a matt or polished finish. '925' and the maker's mark of 'DJ' conjoined and a kangaroo are stamped inside the rim. An advertisement for these gumnut thimbles that appeared in the December 1984 issue of *Australian Women's Weekly* brought the thimbles to the attention of a wider audience. They were only available from Thimble Collections in Melbourne.

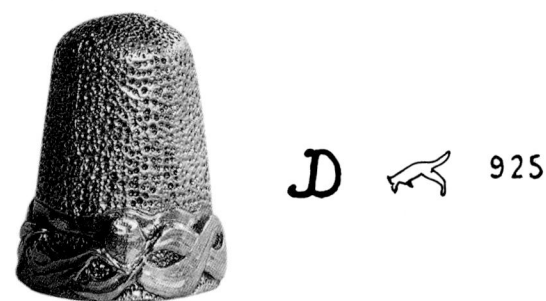

Daniel Jenkins of Melbourne's gumnuts

Rod Kranz

Rod Kranz from South Australia has made silver thimbles. During the 1980s Kranz displayed his silversmithing and so came to the attention of thimble collectors.

The body of his thimbles is smooth and fairly straight-sided. There are two grooves close to the rim. The decoration itself is concentrated near the apex and consists of a band of stylised roses that continues onto the apex. The maker's marks are stamped onto the band, '925' and the initials 'RK' conjoined.

Rod Kranz of South Australia

Zygmunt L

These silver thimbles carry the maker's mark 'ZL' for Zygmunt L, a Polish-born gold and silversmith who arrived in Australia in 1984. Paul Weir, a collector of early Australian silver, who now lives in the Southern Highlands of New South Wales, conceived the designs for the thimbles and went into partnership with Zygmunt making .925 silver thimbles, in response to the demand from Australian collectors for thimbles with Australian motifs.

The thimbles are indented on the apex and for half the body; the rim is rolled. Castings are affixed to the side of these functional, small sized thimbles. The four designs available include koala, wattle, kangaroo and the Sydney Opera House. They are only made in the one size. Some of the thimbles are stamped with the maker's mark 'ZL' in a lozenge and all have '925' in a second lozenge on the band.

Zygmunt L's wattle

Tony Lievesley

Tony Lievesley of the Gold Coast in Queensland handcrafts thimbles of sterling silver. His silver thimbles are made for quilters to use as the hand indented apex is concave. The rest of the thimble is completely plain with two raised rings applied near the apex and another near the rim. '925' is stamped on the band. 'TL' and a consecutive serial number are inscribed inside the rim.

Tony Lievesley of Nerang's quilter's thimble

Tony is an industrial electrician who has turned his hand to stone cutting and faceting, gold and silversmithing. As well as making thimbles, Tony has made a silver medallion, commissioned by the Gold Coast City Council, that went up in the *Challenger* shuttle in 1997.

Irene Marshall

Irene Marshall from Buderim in Queensland, though no longer practising, was a silversmith during the 1970s and 1980s. When she and Joyce Nixon-Smith met in 1980, Joyce persuaded Marshall to try her hand at making silver thimbles. Joyce gave Irene a thimble to base her design and shape upon, and the results were very pleasing. Fewer than six were made, however, as the silversmith felt that the work involved was not worth the return.

They are handmade with an alternating pattern of daisies and dots that continues over the apex. They are stamped inside with '.925 Stg Sil' with no other maker's marks.

Irene Marshall of Buderim

R.P.A. Matho-Dudare

Matho-Dudare is an artist-jeweller, designer and maker of creative jewellery and artefacts in Queensland. He has worked in gold and silver since 1968. His thimbles are handmade and heavy in weight. The top half of the thimble is stippled and there is a plain wide band with a rolled rim. The

R.P.A. Matho-Dudare of Queensland

variety that Matho brings to his thimbles is in the shape and apex. The apex is either hand indented and domed, or flat with ivory from old piano keys or stones set into it. Some have a decorative apex, for example, a dome in the shape of a rose. Since he started making thimbles, more for his pleasure than for a commercial market, Matho has created about fifty thimbles. His thimbles are innovative and never made in quantity, rather as one-off creations.

Matho-Dudare uses several maker's marks. His latest thimbles are marked with 'Matho' in script and a date inside the thimbles and have 'Silver' on the band; marks on some are 'St S' with a conjoined 'MD' in a lozenge; others have 'Matho' in a diamond shaped lozenge.

Ray Norman

Ray Norman, from the Sturt Workshop in Mittagong, New South Wales, made heavy sterling silver thimbles in the mid seventies. They have 'Stg. Sil' and the maker's mark stamped on the band. The thimbles are hand indented, either all over or only on the top half. The rim is rolled. Being handmade, no two of Norman's thimbles are identical.

Ray Norman of Mittagong

Some examples of his thimbles have been found sitting on wooden or marble plinths; some of these are in turn decorated with silver hands, each holding a spool of thread or a needle.

Syd Oates

Syd Oates of Beaufort in Victoria turned silver thimbles over a period of ten years, ceasing about 1994. Originally from England, Oates brought his silver punches with him to Australia. His thimbles are both practical and decorative and have clear

Syd Oates of Beaufort showing an opal apex

maker's marks stamped inside the rim: 'Stg. Sil' in a lozenge, an anchor mark and a stemmed rose, with a size mark. Some of his silver thimbles have good quality white opals or other semi-precious stones as the apex.

The thimbles are highly decorated all over on a smooth background; on some the patterning flows onto the apex, some have intricate applied galleried borders reminiscent of nineteenth century thimble decoration. Several of Oates' thimbles have been available in Ballarat in Victoria, leading collectors to believe erroneously that they were made in Ballarat.

Mrs N. Parker

John Harris & Son is a firm of silversmiths of Perth who specialise in making jewellery and native flowers for their spoons and other small silver items. In 1988 Mrs N. Parker, John Harris' daughter, made a sterling silver thimble with a tiny bunch of gumnuts and gumleaves attached. The body of the thimble is stippled all over, with a plain wide band and a rolled rim. It is not known whether this is a one-off thimble or not.

The very clear maker's marks, consisting of '925' 'N.C.P.' and a date, are stamped inside the rim.

N. Parker of Perth's gumnuts

William Robinson

Bill Robinson of South Australia is a mould maker for chocolates and crafts. He also makes silver charms. Gallery One persuaded Robinson to create silver thimbles and since 1992 he has handmade several. His first design has three silver hopping kangaroos affixed to body. The background has a faint daisy pattern and the apex is indented. His first thimbles were small.

Bill's second design is larger, thimbles with a more defined rounded apex. The indentations, more uniform than on his first thimbles, are on both the body and the apex. Two tiny pairs of scissors are affixed—an appropriate decoration for thimbles to be used by needleworkers.

The third of Robinson's thimbles has the same all-over daisy pattern as his first thimbles. They have two maps of Australia affixed, showing the seven states and territories of the Commonwealth. Australian doublet opals are set into the apex. Robinson's thimbles are the only silver thimbles to have opals incorporated into the design.

All Robinson's thimble designs are inscribed inside the rim with 'WR Australian Made'; '925' is stamped into the band and they are supplied with a leaflet from Gallery One. They are still being produced.

LEFT Bill Robinson of South Australia's scissors thimble
RIGHT Bill Robinson of South Australia, with an opal apex

Tor Schwank

Tor Schwank operated as a silversmith in High Street, Malvern, in Melbourne in the 1970s. Schwank's thimbles are unadorned, with the top half chased to give a stippled effect; there is a plain wide band. His sterling silver thimbles are flared in shape giving good clean lines. They are stamped 'Stg Sil' inside the thimbles, but bear no maker's mark. Schwank's thimbles are no longer produced.

Tor Schwank of Melbourne

James Swann & Son

James Swann & Son made silver thimbles in Birmingham and some were imported from England into Australia by Magnus Goldring Pty Ltd of Sydney from 1950. James Swann & Son has been producing silver thimbles since 1887 and today are the only major English manufacturer still producing silver thimbles. They also produced enamel on silver thimbles after World War II. Initially when enamel thimbles were made, the designs under the enamel would have been handpainted. The Swann enamel designs of the 1970s were produced using high quality decals under the enamel to keep costs down.

Blue wrens are uniquely Australian. 'Blue Wren' is lettered on the verso of these white enamel over sterling silver thimbles. 'J S & S' is stamped up in the apex together with the Birmingham hallmarks. Other Australian birds on enamel thimbles include the same budgerigar design used by Whitehill Silver & Plate Co. (page 41). These were advertised for sale by The Thimble Guild in January 1991 (*Plate 4*).

John Tarasin

John Tarasin, who was especially commissioned to make this sterling silver and gold thimble, is a manufacturing jeweller in Sydney. The decoration is of 9 carat gold and the design is mini gold pillars around the band with a thick gold rim. The rest of the design is abstract engraving. This modern thimble is inscribed '9 ct S/S. JRT for …' inside the

John Tarasin of Sydney's silver and gold thimble

thimble and was made in 1987. This is only one of two examples seen in Australia where gold is used as part of the decoration on silver thimbles.

Ian Trafford-Walker

Ian Trafford-Walker is an artist from the Murwillumbah area of northern New South Wales and nephew of Betty Maloney, the illustrator of this book. He has created two designs in silver and gold thimbles. Ian is well known as the artist who painted the mural on the water tower in Byron Bay in the 1980s. He has had his two designs, one of a kangaroo, the other a lighthouse with a whale, translated into thimbles by silversmiths in Indonesia.

The first advertisement for the sale of his kangaroo design thimbles appeared in the *Thimble Society of London* (autumn 1994): a gold kangaroo affixed to silver thimbles. The Byron Bay Lighthouse thimble is executed in silver with gold decoration of whales. Ornamented in wirework typical of the Indonesian silversmiths, the apex is ornate on the kangaroo thimbles, where the lighthouse thimbles' apex follows the shape of the lighthouse. Only a few have ever been made. There are no maker's marks (*Plate 5*).

Ian Trafford-Walker's Indonesian-made gold on silver kangaroo design

Marylyn Verstraeten

Marylyn Verstraeten was born and educated in Perth, but she now lives and works in Melbourne. Verstraeten's jewellery and sculptures are purchased and commissioned privately by Australian businesses, State and Federal governments as presentations to royalty and visiting dignitaries. She works in silver and gold.

Marylyn Verstraeten has created a range of sterling silver thimbles. Band designs feature two sculptured main figures, with the top half of the thimble and the apex being indented. Her thimbles are engraved 'Australian made' inside the rim and her maker's mark of a conjoined 'MV' and 'Stg Sil' are stamped onto the thimbles in the patterned

Marylyn Verstraeten of Melbourne's kangaroo paw design

section, well hidden in the background of the ornate band.

The thimbles are available in eight designs: kangaroo, koala, Leadbeater's possum, echidna, gumnuts, frill-necked lizard, platypus and kangaroo paw. The thimbles are cast and are currently available only in one size, but Marylyn plans to offer a range of useable sizes.

Marylyn has her studio at the Meat Market Craft Centre in Melbourne.

Malcolm Walter

Malcolm Walter is a gold and silversmith who makes fine quality jewellery. Born in Victoria, he trained as a teacher and taught for nine years. Once he gained his Diploma of Art in gold and silversmithing, he worked in London's Hatton Gardens for nearly four years. On his return to Australia in 1980 he settled in South Australia where he became the Goldsmith in Residence and by Appointment to Birdwood Mill. There he designed and made fine trophies and undertook many commissions.

In 1991 he approached Pan Arts about making silver thimbles. Originally his thimbles were of cast sterling silver, with a 'crown' of cast silver decoration. The only design for these solid silver thimbles is a ring of gumnuts and gumleaves set around the thimbles. Only thirty of these thimbles were ever made. They were sold at too

Malcolm Walter of South Australia's silver gumnuts design

reasonable a price so that Malcolm Walter did not continue to make them in silver. Thereafter the 'crowns' in silver were affixed around German crystal thimbles. See Crystal and Glass thimbles (page 91) for further details.

Malcolm has worked with Australian wooden thimbles since 1993, on which he applies his silver and, more recently, copper and bronze motifs. See Wooden thimbles (page 89).

Walter's silver thimbles are smooth sided with the decoration applied around the thimbles. There are maker's marks for '925', 'MW' conjoined and a hopping kangaroo, each in a lozenge stamped into the silver. The apex is hand indented and the thimbles have a rolled rim.

Whitehill Silver & Plate Co.

The English firm of Whitehill Silver & Plate Co. is well known for making enamel silver thimbles. Amongst their many designs, the thimbles illustrated here have an Australian scene showing two budgerigars amongst wattle on a white background, with the name of the birds lettered on the verso. The silver apex is fairly well domed with the indentations in rings. The thimbles are hallmarked up in the apex for Birmingham with 'WS & P'. These thimbles were made in the 1980s (*Plate 6*).

Comparing the identical designs with budgerigars from James Swann & Son (page 39) and Whitehill Silver & Plate, the latter is of finer quality, with a thicker application of enamel.

COMMEMORATIVE THIMBLES

Commemorative thimbles of the 1950s and 1960s were not made in Australia. For the Royal Visit of Australia by Queen Elizabeth II in 1954, hundreds of Royal commemoratives were made, yet there were no thimbles. The Olympics were hosted by Melbourne in 1956 and similarly no thimbles were produced.

The Bicentenary of Australia in 1988 was the first relatively recent large-scale opportunity for thimblemakers, wholesalers and the like to have commemorative thimbles made. No thimbles bore the Bicentennial logo as any company making items sporting the logo or the word 'Bicentenary' had to pay a levy to the Bicentenary Authority and become an official licensee. With the Olympic Games to be held in Sydney in 2000, however, thimble collectors can look forward to a plethora of Australian souvenir and commemorative thimbles.

With the resurgence of creative handwork of all types, various guilds for embroiderers and quilters have sprung up since the 1960s in Australia. As some of the Guilds reached 20, 21, 25 or 30 years since establishment, it seemed appropriate to have commemorative thimbles commissioned to celebrate the event.

The Embroiderers Guild NSW Inc. commissioned a special silver thimble to commemorate the bicentenary of Australia in 1988. The design was decided upon by a group of Guild members of the Canvas Work class, headed by Prue Socha, their tutor. The design was given to a jeweller to make, but his name remains unknown. The thimble bears an embossed map of Australia with '1788–1988' stamped onto the map; on the verso, the Guild's logo (a threaded needle), is embossed. The apex is nicely domed and indented and the rim is rolled. The thimbles are cast and are quite heavy in weight. There are no maker's marks, but 'Stg Sil' is stamped above the rim in an oblong lozenge, between the two embossed decorations.

The advertisement in the Guild's newsletter *The Record*, of April 1987, does not do the thimbles justice—they are dainty. The same line-drawing advertisement appeared in the July-August issue of *Thimbletter*, a thimble newsletter published in the USA by Lorraine Crosby, and in the July 1987 issue of *TCI Bulletin*. This intensive advertising by the Guild ensured these commemoratives had a worldwide distribution. Two hundred thimbles were manufactured. It is the only thimble the Guild has commissioned. The last of these thimbles was sold in 1996.

Embroiderers Guild of NSW Bicentennial thimble showing Guild logo

As far as can be ascertained these Guild thimbles are the only silver thimbles made to commemorate the Bicentenary of Australia.

OTHER SILVER THIMBLES

These three silver thimbles have no maker's marks but including their photographs may reveal the identity of the silversmiths.

The plain smooth sided thimble at the top has an attractive acanthus leaf decoration on the apex, and a rolled rim. There are no marks.

The thimble in the middle was made in Mittagong, New South Wales—very straight sided with no tapering, unusual in a thimble, with a deeply scalloped edge. A rolled ring bisects the body of the thimble. The apex is stippled with smooth sides. There are no marks.

The third thimble was purchased in Tanunda, South Australia, during 1997. It is handmade with handpunched indentations on the apex and fine decoration, with a rolled rim. There are no marks.

TOP *Silver with acanthus apex—unknown maker*
MIDDLE *Silver made in Mittagong*
BOTTOM *Handmade silver, Tanunda*

Gold thimbles

Australian made gold thimbles are extremely scarce. There are only three known makers. Other than the gold Nifty thimbles, the others were probably made in very small quantities or as one-offs.

George Henry Palfrey

George Henry Palfrey began his career as a jeweller travelling around Victoria in a trap, selling his wares. In 1896 he opened his first jewellery shop at 317 Little Collins Street in Melbourne and traded there until 1923. He moved the business to 17 Howey Place in 1924 where his daughter Stella joined him. Palfrey died in 1927 and Stella continued to operate the business until 1940.

In 1900 Palfrey is listed as 'goldsmith and jeweller; jewellery, watch and clock hospital; expert evaluator'. A search for advertisements about Palfrey's jewellery in *Australian Manufacturing Jewellers, Watchmakers and Opticians Gazette* yielded no results. This would mean that Palfrey was well established enough not to advertise. This is supported by the fact that George Palfrey was known as 'the' jeweller to go to for good jewellery.

Only a few gold thimbles, a gold crochet hook with cover and a gold ribbon threader with George Palfrey's marks on them have been found. All are made of a distinctive 9 carat pink gold, bearing the Palfrey marks on the rim.

There is a wide band with 'Palfrey' lettered in one lozenge. The mark of a horizontal diamond shape, 'F' and '9' are all in one rectangular lozenge, followed by the size mark stamped directly onto the band. On another Palfrey thimble, instead of an 'F', there is a more solid mark that could not be confused with an 'F'. Some of Palfrey's marks are stamped upside down, which has lead to confusion in deciphering them. The thimbles encountered are sizes 8 and 9. The crochet hook and the ribbon threader bear identical Palfrey marks and are completely unadorned (*Plate 7*).

Palfrey's thimbles are the most ornate Australian made thimbles found—daisies within a diamond pattern—giving the thimbles a richness notwithstanding their being gold. This patterning is continued over the apex. The patterning varies slightly on the two known Palfrey thimbles but the basic concept is the same. These are the some of best made thimbles to come out of Australia. They are practical but also have a quiet beauty that reflects the skill of the jeweller.

Two Palfrey marks

Price & Jardine

Price & Jardine are well known for their Nifty products. Mr H.C. Jardine was a firm believer that, when 'the purse was light, as during the Depression years, the aesthetic sense of the public is undiminished'. His judgment in this was accurate, as the 9 carat gold silver-lined jewellery range that Price & Jardine manufactured allowed the community to purchase jewellery with the sentimental value of gold but within the reach of all income groups, not being solid gold.

In April 1923 Price & Jardine introduced their range of 9 carat silver-lined products. Ten years later,

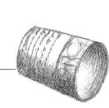

```
PALFREY, GEORGE
  HENRY
  Goldsmith    and    jeweller;
  jewellery,   watch   and   clock
  hospital; expert valuator; 317
  Little   Collins-st,  corner  of
  Block-place
```

Early advertisement for George Palfrey 1900

Page Thirty-eight.   THE COMMONWEALTH JEWELLER AND WATCHMAKER.   October 10, 1936.

For YOUR XMAS TRADE
INSIST ON "NIFTY" PRODUCTS

MADE IN AUSTRALIA

FLEXIBLE WATCH BANDS

FOR LADIES AND GENTS

Large Assortment of Patterns, Finest Finish.

Made in 9ct. Solid Gold, 9ct. Gold with Silver Lining (Guaranteed 5 years), Nickel and Gilt

---

ARMLETS, GOLF BANGLES and FLEXIBLE BANGLES
9ct. Gold, Silver Lined (Guaranteed 5 years)

STUDS, One Piece, 9ct. Gold, 9ct. Silver Lined, Silver and Gilt.

COLLAR PINS, BROOCHES, LINKS, 9ct. Silver Lined.

THIMBLES, 9ct. Silver Lined and Silver, **BOOK MARKERS**

WHOLESALERS ONLY

Support Local Industry   "NIFTY" PRODUCTS
                             431 ELIZABETH STREET - - SYDNEY.

Support the Advertisers Who Support Your Journal.

First mention of the 9 carat silver-lined Nifty thimbles

Left: silver Nifty; right: 9 carat gold silver-plated Nifty, showing the difference with the elliptical ring around the gold Nifty

GOLD THIMBLES

> ## THE STORY OF *Nifty* SILVER LINING
>
> 9CT. GOLD
>
> JOINT FIRMLY SOLDERED UNDER EXTREME PRESSURE
>
> SILVER ALLOY LINING
>
> The Gold and Silver ingots are joined and rolled to gauge under great pressure, giving the plate a hard surface. The Silver Lining gives the Gold added wearing quality. Like Gold, this Silver Lining will not corrode or discolour, and has no harmful effect on the skin.
>
> The quality ratio of the finished article is positive, that is the thickness of the 9ct. in relation to the Silver alloy is as you order. 1/10th or 1/20th quality.
>
> When you sell "NIFTY" Silver Lined Watch Bands or Jewellery you sell "QUALITY."
>
> ## NO OTHER CAN COMPARE
>
> September 10, 1951.   THE COMMONWEALTH JEWELLER AND WATCHMAKER   Page 48E

in an interview in the November 1933 issue of *Commonwealth Jeweller and Watchmaker*, Price & Jardine confirmed that their line of 9 carat silver lined items 'is definitely guaranteed to consist of two plates of 9ct. gold, rolled (not deposited) on to a silver lining following which the two sheets of gold will be found intact . . . also produced in 9ct. silver lined . . . thimbles'. It was not until October 1936 that the above journal carried the first advertisement for Price & Jardine's 9 carat silver lined thimbles.

The gold thimbles bear the marking '9ct Sil lined' and the word 'Nifty' appears either before or following, with a size mark. The difference between the silver and the gold Nifty thimbles is in the word 'Nifty'. On gold thimbles it is enclosed in an elliptical ring. The pattern of the daisies and the two rows of Xs is the same design as on the silver Nifty thimbles (*Plate 8*).

The gold Nifty thimble boxes are a different colour from the boxes for the silver thimbles, being a pale creamy yellow with green lettering. '9 ct Silver Lined "Nifty" Made in Australia' is lettered on the lid (*Plate 9*).

Not many examples of personally engraved Australian thimbles remain; however, three gold Niftys engraved to commemorate special occasions have survived. One has 'To Auntie on her Golden Wedding Day from Marion and Russell 31-1-1892' (that would have been for 1942); another has 'Mother to Beryl 1939' and the third 'EJ November 1939'. Mr Jardine's theory about these 9 carat gold silver lined items being within the reach of the ordinary people for special occasions is borne out by these engraved examples.

Price & Jardine supported the move in New South Wales by the Jewellery Association to have a hallmarking system, to offer a standard of quality. The mark for gold items of jewellery adopted in New South Wales is a kookaburra. The mark would also include the mark for the quality of gold used, e.g. '9.375' for 9 carat gold. From 1923, there was also to be a year of manufacture, starting with a capital A. There was an assay office, the Sydney Hall Mark Company, which did all the testing for the jewellers who sent their gold and silver items for hallmarking. Whether gold or silver, there is only one known thimble that has come to light with a clear example of this hallmarking.

According to the list of the conforming jewellers that appeared in issues of *Commonwealth Jeweller and Watchmaker* in the 1920s, Price & Jardine's mark was 'P.J.P.'.

A single thimble bears this maker's mark of Price & Jardine, together with the hallmarking for New South Wales. A gold thimble, with a waffle design all over and two grooves above a plain band, it has 'P.J.P [size] 10', a kookaburra, '9.375' and 'E' for 1927 on the band. 'P.J.P' and the size mark are stamped directly onto the band whereas the kookaburra and the gold marks are in lozenges. The only variation from the published Price & Jardine mark is that the final fullstop is missing. This gold marked thimble has to be the most significant thimble find in Australia today (*Plate 10*).

A second identically designed thimble exists, but it is only stamped '9^{CT} [size] 10'. A comparison of these two thimbles suggests they could both have been made by the same maker. There is a only slight variation in the way the two grooves have been made. The unmarked gold thimble bears none of the English gold marks for the time, so it can safely be assumed to be a Price & Jardine gold thimble (*Plate 11*).

A third 9 carat gold thimble by Price & Jardine has recently come to light. The bulk of the thimble design is the waffle pattern, similar to the other two. Between the waffle and the plain band, however, there is a well defined single row of daisies. These daisies, with a well defined centre, are identical to those on well struck 9 carat silver lined Nifty thimbles. The marks are '9^{CT} P.J.P [size] 7'. There are no other marks for the New South Wales hallmarking system, which leads one to believe the system had been abandoned by Price & Jardine by the time this thimble was made.

The thimble has been engraved with the initials MAS and the date 25-12-37, a date still within the parameters of Price & Jardine's output (*Plate 12*). If the hallmarked thimble is the most significant thimble in Australia today, this one is prettier!

John Storm

John Storm enjoys jewellery making as a hobby and a modern gold thimble was made by him in Newcastle, New South Wales, in 1995, with an opal set into the thimble. As far as can be ascertained this is a one-off.

Made of yellow gold, the thimble is hand indented on the apex and the top half. The wide band is delicately etched with a fine abstract pattern and there is a rolled rim. The opal set into the side of the thimble has been left unbacked to allow the beauty of the opal to shine through. The thimble is stamped on the inside rim with '9ct' in a lozenge and 'JS' inscribed in cursive and the date it was made (*Plate 13*).

GOLD THIMBLES

| GOLDSMITHS. | JEWELLERS. | SILVERSMITHS. |

The Manufacturing Jewellers' Association of New South Wales

has endorsed

THE AUSTRALIAN HALL MARK

Mr. Wholesaler—   Mr. Retailer—

HALL-MARK YOUR GOODS AND ENSURE QUALITY

SYMBOLS AND MARKS FOR GOLD AND SILVER ADOPTED BY THE AUSTRALIAN HALL

 9 .375    15 .625    18 .75   Silver  .925

The English Hall Mark has withstood the test for 600 years, and is a household word for quality. The Australian Hall Mark standard is as high, being based on exactly similar lines. All Hall-Marked goods are independently assayed by the Australian Hall Mark Company.

MAKE THE AUSTRALIAN HALL MARK THE QUALITY STANDARD OF YOUR HOUSE.

MEMBERSHIP LIST AND REGISTERED MARKS.

MOUNTFORD, FREDK., Swivels, Chains, Jewellery, 130 Sussex Street. (F.M.)

PEARCH, T., Diamond Mounter, 110B Bathurst Street. (T.P.)

JACK BROS., LTD. Manufacturing Jewellers, 152 Strand Arcade. (J.Bs.)

ROWE & SON, Ringmakers, Jewellers, 135 King Street. (R. & Sn.)

SANSOME, E., Chains, Jewellery, 104 Goulburn Street. (E.S.)

CLARKE & WALTON, Manufacturing Jewellers, Douglass Chambers, Wynyard Lane. (C.W.)

DEATON, W. F., Manufacturing Jeweller, 183 Hay Street. (W.F.D.)

FREIZER, F., Manufacturing Jeweller, 21 Market Street. (F.)

GROUT & COY., Manufacturing Jewellers, 178 Castlereagh Street. (G. & Coy.)

FENTON, J. S., Manufacturing Jeweller, 133 Liverpool Street. (J.S.F.)

BELLE, HENRI, Plat. Gold, Silver Chain, 62 Goulburn Street. (H.BL.)

PRICE & JARDINE, LTD., Manufacturing Jewellers, 431 Elizabeth Street. (P.J.P.)

MOUNTFORD, GEO. W., Hollow and Solid Chains, Hill Street, Kogarah, Sydney. (G.W.M.)

COLEMAN & BADDOCK, Goldsmiths, Silversmiths, Cups, Trophies, 8 Gibbons Street, Redfern, Sydney. (C.&B.)

BUCKLEY & MADDAMS, Manufacturing Jewellers, 95 Oxford Street. (B.&M.)

HANMAN, J. H., Manufacturing Jeweller, 454 George Street. (J.H.H.)

TANDY & HARRERS, Manufacturing Jewellers, 522 George Street. (T.&H.)

Further lists of names and registered Marks will appear in subsequent issues.

F. MOUNTFORD, President.   R. W. DICKIE, Secretary, 130 Sussex Street.

The Australian Hall Mark Company was inaugurated for the purpose of having gold and silver goods tested by an independent assayer before distribution.

Australian hallmarks, showing the Price & Jardine mark, P.J.P.

China and porcelain thimbles

With no bone china clay found naturally in Australia, few bone china thimbles have been made here. Many wholesalers, societies and individuals have commissioned English fine bone china companies to produce thimbles for sale with Australian themes. Many of these thimbles bear an Australian backstamp, though they have been made overseas.

China thimbles are not produced to be used for sewing—they are uncomfortable to wear and cannot fit the finger as well as silver or brass thimbles, that with wear gently mould to the shape of the finger. As well, being indented only on the apex limits their usefulness for sewing. The risk of being accidentally dropped during use makes them impractical sewing implements. These thimbles have been made purely for the collectables market from the 1970s onwards.

Many modern china or porcelain thimbles claim to be handpainted. Closer inspection will often reveal that the design is a decal with one or two spots of paint added to the design. Mostly, the word 'handpainted' applies to the gold trim that can only be applied by hand. So technically the thimble is handpainted, but not in the sense that thimble collectors expect. As over 90% of china thimbles have gold bands, only the absence of gold trim will be noted in the following descriptions.

The quantity of thimbles produced is largely influenced by economics. It is unusual to find a run of china thimbles in Australia in quantities under 250.

Ashley Downs

English bone china thimbles with the backstamp of Ashley Downs of Yorkshire were commissioned by Gallery One in May 1992. The designs are all similar, with a wreath of small flowers and the names of selected cities and towns of Australia lettered in gold within the wreath. The cities include Beechworth, Bright, Fingal, Fremantle, Hobart, Melbourne, Perth WA, Swansea in Tasmania, Sydney, and have the backstamp 'Ashley Downs English Fine Bone China'. Between 10 and 60 thimbles were made for each town or city.

Ashley Downs of England's Perth thimble

Australian Collectors Treasury

Australian Collectors Treasury produced boxed sets of seven thimbles portraying State wildflowers. The thimbles were made in Japan. The designs include: Victoria (pink heath), Northern Territory (Sturt's desert rose), New South Wales (waratah), Tasmania (flowering gum), South Australia (Sturt's desert pea), Queensland (Cooktown orchid), Western Australia (kangaroo paw). The thimbles only have the name of the State lettered on them while the names of the flowers are on labels in the accompanying box. The thimbles have no backstamp. The boxes are blue and rectangular with 'Australian Collectors Treasury' lettered on the inside lid. A leaflet supplied with the thimbles gives a brief history of thimbles and a description of the flowers.

Series of seven wildflowers by Australian Collectors Treasury

The thimbles were only available in the 1980s by mail order through Bond International Pty Ltd in Sydney. A similar set of six was available with New Zealand wildflowers.

Australian Impressions

Australian Impressions Fine Bone China thimbles were designed by Gallery One in Perth in 1988, and were made in 1989 in England by Victoria Jane Bone China. There are eighteen designs in the series and 1000 of each design were made. The fauna and Western Australian thimbles have 'Australian Impressions Fine Bone China' as the backstamp inside.

AUSTRALIAN IMPRESSIONS
FINE BONE CHINA

The first group comprises six State fauna emblems: red kangaroo, Northern Territory; Leadbeater's possum, Victoria; numbats, Western Australia; koalas, Queensland (K1); platypus, New South Wales; wombat, South Australia. The thimbles have the backstamp inside the rim.

State floral emblems is the second group and comprises nine designs: golden wattle, Australia; waratah, New South Wales; kangaroo paw, Western Australia; Cooktown orchid, Queensland; Sturt's desert pea, South Australia; Sturt's desert rose, Northern Territory; royal bluebell, Australian Capital Territory; pink heath, Victoria; Tasmanian blue gum, Tasmania. The backstamp is printed on the verso of the thimbles and the name of the flower is incorporated into the backstamp.

Being based in Western Australia, Gallery One commissioned a third group of thimbles of three local designs: Perth, Western Australia, showing the city from the Swan River; the Round House at Fremantle, which was the State's first gaol, and the black swan, Western Australia's emblem.

Birchcroft Fine Bone China

Birchcroft Fine China was founded in Longton in Stoke-on-Trent by Tony Forbes around 1982. Birchcroft is now the largest manufacturer of china thimbles in the world. Thimbles by Birchcroft are commissioned by Pan Arts Collectables of Sydney. Usually they have a Pan Arts backstamp but some have slipped through with the Birchcroft backstamp.

Pan Arts, as an official sesquicentennial licensee, commissioned two thimble designs from Birchcroft to commemorate Sydney's Sesquicentenary in 1992 as part of their Australia Series. Time was of the essence and these thimbles arrived from Birchcroft with their backstamp instead of that of Pan Arts. 'Series No 28' and 'Series No. 29' (the marks used on all the other Pan Arts Australia Series) still appears on the verso of the thimbles. The first design incorporates the Sydney Opera House, the Harbour Bridge and a multicoloured array of celebratory symbols. The Sesquicentenary logo with the dates '1847–1992' are on the verso. The second is the Sydney Town Hall in monochrome sepia and this has the Sydney coat of arms on the verso.

Birchcroft has also produced thimbles for Norfolk Island including those with a map of the

Australian Impressions Western Australian designs showing the Round House, black swan and Perth

LEFT *Birchcroft's Sydney Sesquicentenary 1992 made for Pan Arts Australia Series No. 28*
RIGHT *One of Birchcroft's Norfolk Island designs*

island in yellow. Tourism plays a huge role in Norfolk Island's economy and several styles and producers of tourist thimbles have been used for sale on this historic island 1700 kilometres north-east of Sydney (K2).

The Cabochon Collection
The designs with an elaborate backstamp for The Cabochon Collection, Hahndorf, Australia, are prduced on blank thimbles from Taiwan, known as 'Taiwan blanks' amongst the thimble collecting fraternity. The decal design has two children in German national costume with 'Hahndorf' lettered on the rim. These are the only Australian thimbles with a backstamp on Taiwan blanks! The lettering is 'The Cabochon Collection' 'Hahndorf Australia'. Examples of this decal design exist for other towns in Australia, but none of them bear the Cabochon backstamp.

Cabochon Collection is the trade name of Eva and Peter Hine of Hahndorf in South Australia, distributors for all the collectables with the German children design.

Cabochon of Hahndorf

Caverswall China
Caverswall Bone China of Longton in Stoke-on-Trent in England produced a whole range of Australian thimbles. Caverswall started producing thimbles in 1973, as a result of the demand worldwide for collectors' thimbles. John Chown who owned Caverswall made thimbles from 1973 until 1993. Caverswall thimbles have always had a distinctive shape. Shorters of Clarence Street in Sydney, purveyors of fine china, were the Australian agents for Caverswall. The Australian thimbles were commissioned by Frank Shorter of Shorters in the late 1970s and 1980s.

LEFT *Caverswall's London Court Perth design*
RIGHT *Caverswall's Brisbane City Hall for Merrol Palmer*

Caverswall is renowned for its thimble series, and several series were commissioned by Shorters. The Capital Cities of Australia series appears not to have been made all at the same time, as some of the Capital City thimbles have more than one symbol: Adelaide—(State theatre/Sturt's Statue); Canberra (Old) Parliament House; Hobart Tasmania—Bridge; Melbourne—Flinders Street Station; Perth—(London Court)/black swan; Sydney—(Harbour Bridge)/waratah. Some of the designs incorporate the name of the icon; the brackets indicate where the name is missing.

In 1988, with the absence of fine china thimbles made in Australia, Merrol Palmer, the proprietor of Shop 12 in Brisbane, commissioned Caverswall to make thimbles with the Brisbane City Hall on them. The design is a sepia decal of the City Hall, with 'Brisbane City Hall' on the verso. Five hundred thimbles were commissioned. This design completes the series of seven Capital Cities. When Sallyanne Atkinson was Lord Mayor of Brisbane in the late 1980s, she used these thimbles as giveaways to promote the City of Brisbane. Though Shop 12 has closed the thimbles are still available in Brisbane.

A series of six thimbles with Australian fauna was made by Caverswall in the early 1980s, featuring kangaroo, platypus, koala (K3), echidna, possum and wombat. The name of each animal appears on the verso.

Another set, of five on this occasion, is the Australian State flowers series with a map of Australia depicting the relevant state on the verso: kangaroo paw, Western Australia; pink heath, Victoria; flowering blue gum, Tasmania; waratah, New South Wales; Sturt's desert pea, South Australia. Each state flower is identified on the verso.

China and Porcelain Thimbles

Caverswall's series of five Australian wildflowers

A final set of five Australian wildflower thimbles is quite different, moving away from the usual State flowers: Menzies banksia, silver wattle, black-eyed Susan, crimson bottlebrush and Christmas bells make up the set. The names of the wildflowers are lettered on the verso.

Shorters also commissioned Caverswall to produce special commemorative thimbles.

In 1980 the Exhibition Building in Melbourne celebrated its centenary. The Building opened on 1 October 1880 for the first Great Exhibition to be held in Australia. No thimbles were made at the time to commemorate the event. The centenary thimbles portray the Exhibition Building in monochrome with 'Melbourne Exhibition 1880–1980' on the verso. The design was taken from a nineteenth century woodcut of the building. These were the first Australian commemorative thimbles commissioned and 1000 were made.

Caverswall's Melbourne Exhibition 1880–1980

In 1983, the Australian yacht *Australia II* won the America's Cup for the first time since its inception in 1851. Caverswall China made thimbles commemorating the event. The thimbles show *Australia II* in colour, with the silver America's Cup on the verso and the words '*Australia II*'. The thimbles would have been produced at very short notice but they were made to take advantage of the groundswell of national fervour sweeping the country after Australia won the America's Cup.

Prince Charles and Diana, Princess of Wales, made a Royal Visit to Australia in 1983. Caverswall was the only thimblemaker to issue commemorative thimbles for the event, which would

LEFT Caverswall's *Australia II 1983*
RIGHT Caverswall's *Royal Visit 1983*

largely have been to cash in on the popularity of the Royal couple in the early 1980s. The decal shows them with their son Prince William with the words 'Royal Visit Australia & New Zealand March, April 1983' on the verso. Fewer than 1000 thimbles were made.

It is surprising that although Caverswall was still producing thimbles in 1988 they made no Bicentennial thimbles.

All Caverswall thimbles have the backstamp 'Caverswall England' inside and are supplied in Caverswall cardboard thimble boxes with an explanatory leaflet. Caverswall thimbles are no longer being made in England but stocks of the Australian thimbles are still available in Australia.

Franklin Mint Porcelain

Throughout the 1980s Franklin Mint of Philadelphia USA issued limited sets of porcelain thimbles. Those for the Australian market were only sold by subscription on mail order through Franklin Porcelain in Melbourne at the rate of one a month. Two sets have Australian relevance.

The Baby Animals of the World series was issued on behalf of the World Wildlife Fund in 1982. The sets consist of 25 thimbles. The thimbles are of the distinctive tall, highly domed shape associated with Franklin Mint and are embellished with 22 carat gold. Only two of the baby

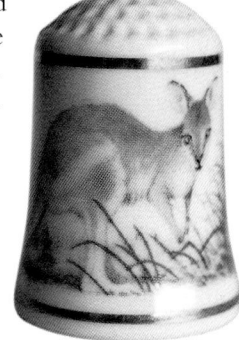

Franklin Mint's baby wallaby

animals in the series are Australian, the koala (K4) and the sandy wallaby.

The backstamp reads 'Franklin Center Penn-sylvania 19019'. On the verso of the thimbles are the copyright date of 1981 and 'WWF'. A certificate of authenticity with each thimble identifies Peter Barrett as the original designer. Each thimble also has a descriptive leaflet for each baby animal in the set.

In 1984, Franklin Mint issued series of advertising thimbles. There is a series known as The General Store Thimbles for American products and a range for Australia. The Australian range consists of sets of 25 porcelain thimbles, sporting Australian advertisements. None of the advertisements in this series is the same as those that appeared on the aluminium advertising thimbles of the 1920s and 1930s (pages 67–74). The sets have an accompanying booklet giving a history of each Australian product. Australians will identify with these familiar names: Aeroplane Jelly, Allen's Steam Rollers, Arnott's Biscuits, Chesty Bond Athletics, Clag Paste, ETA Peanut Butter, Hutton's Ham and Bacon, IXL Jam, Jaffas, Kiwi Boot Polish, McAlpin's Flour, Mermaid Salt, Minties, Quaker Oats, Robur Tea, Rosella Tomato Sauce, Sao Biscuits, Schweppes Soda Water, Solvol, Sunlight Soap, Sylko Thread, Tarax, Tom Piper, Tucker Box Dog & Cat Food, Vegemite, Vincent's Powders. How were the 25 products chosen, and by whom? A notable absence is Bushells Tea. The thimbles bear the Franklin Mint backstamp.

Impress Ceramics of Phillip Island

thimble to be produced by Impress Ceramics. The thimbles have a backstamp for 'Impress Ceramics' which includes the address 'Cowes Phillip Island Vic. 3922 Australia'. The thimbles were supplied in gold soft cardboard boxes with 'Australia's Golden Heritage Collection' lettered on the top and 'Handcrafted and decorated in 22 carat gold by Impress Ceramics' on the base. This was in 1988. Phillip Island off the coast of Victoria is famous for its fairy penguin parades.

Impress Ceramics showed enterprise in creating these thimbles for tourists visiting the penguins on Phillip Island and one wonders what happened to them after the super packaging and presentation of this design, as Impress Ceramics ceased to trade after 1989.

Kyneton Fine China

Originally from England, Rita and Peter Daniel settled in Kyneton in Victoria in 1983. There they founded the Kyneton Fine China Studio in 1987 where, under the name of Wattle Ceramics, they produce fine resin sculptures, capturing the essence of Australian fauna and flora. Peter has the flair for flower making and making moulds and Rita is an artist of exceptional talent, having started in the Royal Worcester training school at the age of 17 and ending up being commissioned by Royal Doulton to paint individual works of art on bone china plaques, using the Minton trademark.

In 1995 Kyneton Fine China launched a range of bone china thimbles. Using bone china clay imported from England, the thimbles are made in Kyneton, certainly a first for modern thimbles in Australia.

The thimbles all have a painted dark blue background (except for the blue wren), with a gold

Franklin Mint's General Store series, with four Australian advertisements

Impress Ceramics

As far as can be ascertained, this design of a gold penguin in relief on a ceramic thimble was the only

band on the top and the rim, and are handpainted, originally by Rita Daniel and more recently by Rachel Dettmann. Though the same blue colour is used throughout their thimble range, each thimble is of a slightly different shade. The actual handpainted designs also vary slightly from thimble to thimble. Each design is limited to 100 thimbles and each is numbered, signed ('RD' for Rita Daniel and 'rd' for Rachel Dettmann) and boxed, with a certificate of authenticity that in turn bears the artist's signature and the number in the series. The thimbles have the backstamp 'Kyneton Fine China Made in Australia'.

Kyneton Fine China
MADE IN AUSTRALIA

The current range includes blue wren (on both white and blue backgrounds), robin, daffodil (Kyneton has an annual Daffodil Festival), pansy, poppy and wattle. Kyneton Fine China also produce annual thimbles—gumnuts for the 1996 design—and the year is painted on each thimble (*Plate 14*).

Kyneton Fine China makes an ideal place to start an Australian thimble collection. Owning one of each thimble in the range, with the combination of a limited edition and being handpainted, with an annual thimble being added to the range, or being added to as demand grows, should be incentive enough for collectors old and new.

The studio is open to the public during office hours, where one can see the artists at work. It will be a worthwhile experience for thimble collectors who visit this historic town in the Central Victorian Highlands.

Liberty Lane

The Queen Victoria Building (QVB), built in 1898 in the heart of Sydney, was once used as the city's produce markets. In 1986 this wonderfully restored Victorian building was re-opened as an exclusive shopping area. In 1988 Liberty Lane, a giftshop within the QVB, commissioned thimbles portraying this distinctive Sydney landmark. These thimbles have a maroon decal showing the dome of the building with the letters 'QVB' underneath, on two

Liberty Lane of Sydney's Queen Victoria Building

sides. There is a backstamp for 'Liberty Lane Australia' inside. The decal design was made for Liberty Lane by Westminster China of Victoria using the distinctive blanks they import from China.

Pan Arts Collectables

When Dick and Ann Wallace went into the wholesale thimble business in Sydney in the 1970s, there were no thimbles being produced for collectors in Australia. Initially they imported thimbles from all over the world and were known as Pan Arts Importing. The Wallaces are dedicated to promoting Australia, especially on thimbles, and being passionate about Australia's wildlife, they embarked on a search for Australian theme thimbles to wholesale.

Finding that there were no bone china thimbles available in Australia, around 1985 Dick and Ann commissioned a series of bone china thimbles with Australian designs from Ken Parry and then from Birchcroft Fine China in England. The backstamp on all their thimbles is 'English Bone China Pan Arts Collectables Sydney'. The early Ken Parry thimbles have a plainer backstamp, 'Pan Arts Collectables Sydney - Australia English Bone China'. All the artwork is conceived and designed by Ann Wallace.

Birchcroft   Ken Parry

Backstamps on Pan Arts thimbles

The first series by Pan Arts bears the name 'Australia Series' with a map of Australia, and the number within the series, on the verso. All the designs are multicoloured. The series presently numbers 39 but the range is being added to all the time. Only two (Nos 1 and 6) in the Australia Series are made by Ken Parry (K5, K6, K7). See Appendix 4 for the full listing of the Australia Series (page 116).

Three designs in this series were designed for Australia's Bicentenary in 1988. Pan Arts were official licensees for the Bicentenary. The first commemorative design (No. 13 in the Australia Series) is 'Advance Australia Fair 1788–1988': two Australian flags with wattle spilling around them. The second is 'Bound for Australia 1788' (No. 15 of the Australia Series) in two different colours, 11 blue ships or 11 yellow ships, representing the First Fleet. The final in the Bicentennial trio is No. 16 in the Australia Series, 'Sydney Cove–1788' depicting the landing. All designed by Ann Wallace, each design celebrates something special in the founding of Australia.

Pan Arts Australia Series 15, 13 and 16 for the Bicentenary

A second series bearing the Pan Arts backstamp is the Signature Series. This series of twelve Australian birds is multicoloured. The bird designs were compiled by Ann Wallace. These thimbles were marketed by Magnamail in 1989 and could be bought singly or as a series. A full list appears in Appendix 4 (page 116).

In 1990, another series was marketed by Pan Arts: the WWF Australia Series for the World Wide Fund for Nature. The artwork was researched and drawn by Ann Wallace; her designs had to be approved by the WWF before the thimbles could bear the WWF panda symbol on the verso. A percentage of all sales went to the WWF. The series represents Australian Endangered Species and contains 25 thimbles covering 66 species that are endangered in Australia. Only 250 sets were made. Examples of this series exist with the Birchcroft backstamp, but these would only be available in England through Birchcroft.

Pan Arts Endangered Species series showing five of the designs

Ann Wallace spent nearly a year researching the endangered Australian creatures that are featured on the Pan Arts sculptured resin series of thimbles. One can capture exquisite detail with resin and there were only fifty of each thimble made in this series. Though originally conceived as a set of twelve thimbles, only ten were sold by Pan Arts in Australia. The sculptures were created from Ann's drawings by Tony Barnes of Rydale in England. Each resin sculpture is handpainted and affixed to plain china thimbles. These thimbles were also Australian World Wide Fund for Nature thimbles and bear their WWF Australia logo on the verso; they are the Endangered and Threatened Species range, issued in 1990. See Appendix 4 (page 116) for the full range, including colourful butterflies.

Pan Arts also have a Special Series. These are custom designed thimbles for events and places and are only available from the outlets which commissioned the thimbles. They are a numbered series, e.g. S15; where the number is included on the thimble, a

Pan Arts Endangered and Threatened Species resin butterfly

map of Australia and the relevant number appear on the verso. For a full listing of the range available, see Appendix 4. Some of the thimbles in this Special Series call for further mention. *The Sun-Herald* Koala Fund thimbles are number S4. *The Sun-Herald* newspaper in Sydney used to have a Koala Fund 'dedicated to the survival of the koala'. In early 1989 Pan Arts and *The Sun-Herald* jointly produced thimbles for fundraising purposes. The artist was Celia Johnson and 500 thimbles were made (K8). A needlework-related thimble was commissioned for the Melbourne Quilt Exhibition in 1992. The design is quite simple in monochrome but is eagerly sought after by thimble collectors. Though not numbered on the thimbles, these thimbles are number S12 in the Special Series. Queensland Quilters have commissioned the most recent in the Pan Arts Special Series. The design has their logo, of a Queensland house within a red Q, on the front and gum blossoms and '1997' on the verso. Though number S20 in the series, this number does not appear on the thimbles. Only 250 were made and these will be available from Queensland Quilters until stocks are exhausted.

Collectors will also come across Pan Arts thimbles which have the Pan Arts backstamp but which do not have Australian themes.

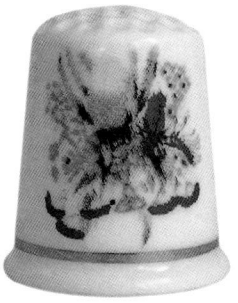

Platypus Gallery's Australian Wild Flowers

LEFT *Pan Arts Special issue for Melbourne Quilt Exhibition 1992*
RIGHT *Pan Arts Special issue for Queensland Quilters 1997*

Platypus Gallery
Vale Fine China was founded in 1986 as a cottage industry in the Vale of Glamorgan in South Wales. In 1996 Platypus Gallery of Melbourne chose Vale for their first design. The thimbles portray two koalas (K1). They have the backstamp for Platypus Gallery and 250 were made. The latest design for Platypus Gallery from Vale Fine China has a colourful bouquet of Australian wildflowers with 'Australian Wild Flowers' lettered on the verso.

Regal Fine Bone China
Regal China of England issued multicoloured sets of six thimbles showing endangered or threatened species of the world, made in the late 1980s. One Australian animal is included in the set—the koala (K3). The thimble shape is the same distinctive shape as those by Caverswall, so one must presume that these were made by Caverswall, especially when the decals are signed by W.R. Tipton, one of Caverswall's top artists. The backstamp reads 'Regal Fine Bone China England'.

Reutter Porcelain
Many thimbles have been made in Germany for the Australian market but it is unusual to find them made of German porcelain. Reutter Porcelain, near Stuttgart, founded in the 1950s by Willy and Maria Reutter, is one of the largest porcelain thimble makers in Germany today.

Reutter have made these Norfolk Island thimbles with Norfolk Island pines as the design. The backstamp is 'Reutter Porzellan Germany'.

Reutter of Germany's Norfolk Island design

Royal Grafton Bone China

Royal Grafton of England first started producing bone china ware in 1876. They have produced thimbles since the 1980s and are now part of the Royal Doulton group.

May Gibbs, the well known illustrator and writer of Australian children's books, had her first books published in 1917; they are still in print today. In 1994 Royal Grafton Bone China made a range of nursery china featuring May Gibbs' Gumnut Babies. Included in the range are thimbles showing two of these Gumnut Babies. The designs incorporate the words 'Gumnut Babies' and 'May Gibbs'. The backstamp includes 'Original Australian Artwork from the works of May Gibbs'.

Both the thimbles are attractively packaged in thimble boxes, with 'Grandmother's thimble' and 'Made in England for J.D. Milner & Associates a wholly owned Australian Company' on the colourful accompanying leaflet.

Royal Grafton's Gumnut Babies 1994

Funds from the sale of these products go to the New South Wales Society for Children with Physical Disabilities and The Spastic Centre of New South Wales. The thimbles are still available from Nutcote, May Gibbs' historic home at Neutral Bay in Sydney.

Royal Worcester Fine Bone China

Royal Worcester, of Worcester in England, stopped producing thimbles in 1984, thus ending a long tradition of thimble making that stretched back into the mid-nineteenth century. Their handpainted porcelain thimbles of the last century and the early twentieth are miniature works of art. Apprentices who were to become Royal Worcester artists served a seven-year apprenticeship; during this period they did not sign their work. Royal Worcester thimbles from about 1900 to the 1950s can be dated from the puce mark inside the thimbles and the system of dating by coded dots within this mark.

Examples of Royal Worcester thimbles from the 1920s have been found in Australia, decorated with handpainted kookaburras. These birds could not be confused with the kingfisher, which is smaller and more brightly coloured bird.

In the May 1994 *Needlework Tool Collectors Society of Australia Newsletter* Edwin Holmes' letter, about a just-discovered Royal Worcester thimble with a handpainted kookaburra, was published. The thimble has a puce mark for 1929 and though not signed, Holmes felt the painting could be ascribed to either of two Royal Worcester painters, Reginald or Walter Austin. These brothers, who were naturalists, specialised in painting Australasian flowers and birds. The kookaburra sitting amidst wattle is quite small on this thimble and is facing to the right; there is a spray of handpainted wattle on the verso. For Holmes the thimble was remarkable for another reason. The unpainted portion has an indented panel in the porcelain on both sides which has been left unglazed. Because of the kookaburra Edwin Holmes felt that this thimble belonged in Australia and in 1994 he sent it to a Australian collector—a most generous gesture (*Plate 15*).

Christie's of London held an auction of thimbles in December 1997 and it was a delight to find an identical Royal Worcester kookaburra thimble for sale, with the same strange unglazed sides. This unsigned, handpainted thimble also dates from 1929.

The first kookaburra thimble, particularly because of the unglazed indented portions on the sides, could have been presumed to be a one-off. The appearance of an identical thimble gives rise to speculation about the indented sides—these have not previously been noted on Royal Worcester thimbles.

Another handpainted Royal Worcester kookaburra thimble, dated 1926, discovered in Australia, was probably painted by an apprentice, as it is unsigned. The kookaburra is very different from the 1929 one and cannot be ascribed to the Austin brothers. The artist would probably never have seen a kookaburra before painting this bird but it is a more realistic size in proportion to the thimble than the kookaburras on the thimbles ascribed to the Austins. The bird is facing to the left amidst a spray of wattle; again there is a spray of wattle on the verso. This thimble belongs in a Royal Worcester cardboard thimble box and is doubly important as the name of the jewellery firm, 'Flavelle, Sankey & Roberts Ltd Sydney Brisbane Rockhampton Lismore' is stamped on the inside lid (*Plate 16*).

According to Landis (1996), Flavelle Bros were known for their strong ties with Royal Worcester.

Spode Bone China

Josiah Spode began making bone china ware in England in 1800. The first Spode thimbles appeared for the collectables market in 1974 and though the company was absorbed by Royal Worcester in 1986 a few Spode thimble issues appeared sporadically until 1992. Spode thimbles are elegant thimbles of quality; most of them have a floral self-patterned apex.

The Embroiderers Guild Victoria chose Spode thimbles to celebrate their 21st birthday in 1981. These custom designed commemorative thimbles have the floral patterned apex, the Embroiderers Guild logo in a distinctive deep green shade on the front and green threads forming a frame around '1981' on the verso. The thimbles are lettered around the rim with 'Embroiderers Guild, Victoria'. Approximately 200 thimbles were made for the Guild and they bear the Spode backstamp on the inside.

Spode's Embroiderers Guild Victoria 1981

Sutherland China

Sutherland China of Stoke-on-Trent in England was established in 1981 by experienced workers from Spode and Wedgwood, and for the next fifteen years they produced thimbles with a distinctive shape with a pointed apex. Sutherland China was commissioned by The Thimble Guild to produce thimbles for Australia's Bicentenary in 1988. John Ball, who is the designer for Sutherland China, conceived these fine thimbles that also commemorated the visit to Australia of the Prince and Princess of Wales.

The thimbles show the Sydney Opera House and the Sydney Harbour Bridge in a wraparound design with 'To celebrate the Australian Bicentenary and the Visit of the Prince & Princess of Wales' lettered around them. The thimbles have the backstamps for both Scotland Direct, the trading name of The Thimble Guild, and Sutherland China. The issue was limited to 1988 thimbles.

Sutherland's Bicentennial Royal Visit 1988

Vale Fine China

Vale Fine China is in Wales. It was established in 1986 as a cottage industry producing thimbles, figures, cottages and boxes in small runs. Vale have proved themselves as producers of neat, well indented, good quality china thimbles.

In 1997 the Country Women's Association (CWA) of Western Australia commissioned fundraising thimbles by Vale through Gallery One Thimbles. Their earlier fundraising thimbles were Australian designed. Both thimble designs have the blue logo of the CWA—'For Home and Country'. These thimbles bear the Vale backstamp.

Vale's Country Women's Association

Wedgwood

Josiah Wedgwood first produced his famous porcelain in England in 1759. The first modern Jasperware thimbles were manufactured in 1980, in Barlaston in the English Potteries, in the familiar Wedgwood blue colour, to commemorate the 250th anniversary of the birth of Josiah Wedgwood in 1730. The bas-reliefs, applied to the bisqueware thimbles in a contrasting colour, are taken from a mould and applied to the body of the thimbles by hand. Wedgwood has only produced one thimble design with an Australian theme.

In 1985 the Wedgwood Collectors Society in Australia had several pieces produced to commemorate the 150th anniversary of the founding of Victoria. The pieces included miniature plates, eggs and miniature vases, all bearing the State flower of Victoria, the pink heath. This was such a successful venture that a thimble design was commissioned. In 1990 the Wedgwood Collectors Society in Castle Hill, New South Wales, had dusty pink Jasperware thimbles made for distribution in Australia with the same 1985 design of the pink heath. These were produced in a limited edition of 2500 which was fully subscribed.

The bas-relief of pink heath is in white. The thimbles are simply stamped 'Wedgwood' on the verso (*Plate 17*). These pink heath thimbles of elegant simplicity were supplied in the usual flat square cardboard Wedgwood thimble boxes, with a sticker with 'T.W.C.S.' on the side.

Westminster China

This Australian company first started decorating china in 1954. As decal specialists, Westminster China develop designs and print their decals in Australia, for placing on porcelain items. This is done by firing in a continuous tunnel kiln. Porcelain blanks imported from China are decorated in Australia with these high quality decals.

This Melbourne based company has produced decals for thimbles from the 1980s. The squarish shape of their thimbles is quite distinctive. The thimbles in their Wildflower series have a backstamp inside for 'Westminster Australia' that incorporates the name of the State for each flower. They are boxed in distinctive square flat maroon cardboard boxes. The thimble designs match other china items, such as mugs, bells and dishes produced by the company.

Australian Wildflowers, their primary range, includes nine designs: blue leschenaultia; Cooktown orchid, Queensland; flowering blue gum, Tasmania; kangaroo paw, Western Australia; pink heath, Victoria; Sturt's desert pea, South Australia; Sturt's desert rose, Northern Territory; waratah, New South Wales; and wattle—a combination of the States' floral emblems and other Australian wildflowers. The name of the flowers is lettered on each thimble. All but the blue leschenaultia thimbles are still in production.

Koala and kangaroo designs are also made by Westminster China (K4). They are quite stark with just the decal applied. The backstamp has 'Fine China Westminster Australia' and is very similar to the Wildflower backstamp.

The most recent design (1997) from Westminster is their 'Tribal Man', an Aboriginal design. The all around design uses authentic Aboriginal art in earth tones of various shades of brown in a traditional dot design. The backstamp is the most comprehensive yet observed on a thimble and has 'Westminster Fine China Designed & Decorated in Australia. Blank made in China © 1995 Tobwabba Art Authentic Aboriginal Art Tribal Man - G 2571'. Westminster China have gone to great lengths in this addition to their range to identify the thimbles as being from offshore, but also to establish the authenticity of the Aboriginal art work.

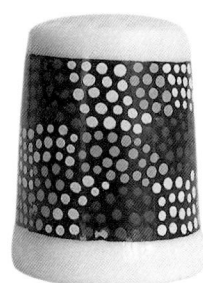

Westminster's Tribal Man with Tobwabba Art

White Heron China

White Heron China in New Zealand make fine quality thimbles. One design with an Australian connection has surfaced. Whether this is part of a set or single thimbles, these 'Kangaroo Paw WA' thimbles are worthy of inclusion in any collection. The thimbles were produced

Westminster of Melbourne's series of seven wildflowers

in the 1980s. The design is plain and uncluttered, with a single spray of kangaroo paw with 'WA' lettered on the verso. The backstamp inside the thimbles has 'White Heron Bone China New Zealand'.

White Heron of New Zealand's kangaroo paw

HANDPAINTED THIMBLES

Porcelain painting has a large following in Australia. Miniature painting, on thimbles especially, requires great skill. Australian fauna is a difficult subject to capture accurately in miniature so one tends in the main to find floral handpainted thimbles. Artists have been encouraged to sign their works and signed handpainted thimbles are eagerly sought after. The blank thimbles used in china painting tend to be squat in shape with a matt finish and are imported from Japan and Czechoslovakia.

The porcelain painters listed here have made an impact on thimble collections in Australia (for a further listing see Appendix 3, page 115). For other miniaturists' handpainted thimbles, see the section on Wooden thimbles (page 85).

Pat Adam

Pat Adam of Adelaide is a china painter of some renown. Her fine brushwork of mini flowers and native animals is often found on thimbles (K9). Pat was commissioned to paint the club thimbles for the South Australian Digitabulists Society in 1990. Jack Turner, the founder of SADS, helped with the design. The thimbles have a posy of Sturt's desert pea, South Australia's floral emblem, and wattle. 'S.A.D.S. Est 1988 South Australia' is lettered on the back of each thimble. The thimbles are signed on the inside rim 'P Adam S.A.'. The off-white porcelain blanks were made by Dorothy Andrews of Paris Creek Pottery.

South Australian Digitabulists Society thimble handpainted by Pat Adam

Gerald Delaney

Gerald E. Delaney is one of the foremost ceramic artists in the United Kingdom today. Delaney spent long periods in Australia in the 1980s and the early 1990s and painted many thimbles during his stay. Gerald was born in 1933 in England. He studied art at the Worcester Victoria Institute and served a seven-year apprenticeship with the Royal Worcester Porcelain Company between 1948 and 1954; he returned to Royal Worcester in 1971 until 1973. He specialised initially in fruit designs. He has enlarged his range to include birds, animals and landscapes and does special commissions. He now travels the world holding workshops where he lectures and gives instruction.

The thimbles illustrated, examples of his much sought after work, show the Australian kookaburra and the lyrebird. A feature of Delaney's work is the gold-painted apex. In 1990 the David Jones store in Sydney had Delaney's thimbles, depicting fruit, for sale. His thimbles are unsigned but bear a backstamp with 'Hand-painted by G. Delaney' (*Plate 18*).

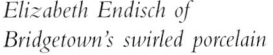

Gerald Delaney's handpainted lyrebird

Elizabeth Endisch

Elizabeth Endisch, who lives at Bridgetown in Western Australia, is very well known for her porcelain work. Elizabeth makes porcelain collector's plates and hand decorates them. Her best known design is based on the Aboriginal dot style. With some persuasion from Sue Gowan, Endisch made porcelain thimbles for the first time in 1989. These were an

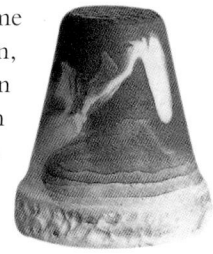

Elizabeth Endisch of Bridgetown's swirled porcelain

experiment using her dot design but they were so time consuming that only four were ever made. Her porcelain thimbles now have a swirled pattern to them. The shape is distinctive with markedly sloping sides and a raised rim. Initially Endisch's thimbles had her maker's mark of a large 'E' painted on the inside. Her later thimbles have no maker's marks.

G. Kedzierska

Just to see these porcelain thimbles or other items being handpainted by Kedzierska makes it worth visiting the weekend markets in The Rocks in Sydney. These fine quality thimbles are made by Kedzierska and their delicate pastel colours enhance the all-over floral painting. The apex is indented and domed and the indentations are highlighted with fine dots of paint. The thimbles are lettered on the inside rim with 'Handpainted by G K Sydney Australia'.

Kedzierska of Sydney's handpainted porcelain

Jan Milton

This talented Adelaide miniaturist has captured several typically Australian themes or icons on thimbles. Aside from the distinctive painting style, one can recognise Jan Milton's thimbles by the gold painted apex.

Themes on Jan's handpainted thimbles include Bennelong, an Aborigine from the Sydney area at the time of European settlement of Australia. Jan has surrounded his portrait with a gilt frame and the name 'Bennelong' is lettered underneath. Jan's country and rural scenes usually include a gum tree; there is Crocodile Dundee showing a crocodile; the Swagman with his billy boiling, and Ned Kelly; all these designs are handpainted all around the thimble. Her Rookwood designs in ochres and reds have gum blossoms and gumnuts; her bush scenes reflect the colours of the Australian bush.

Milton also has painted pairs of thimbles, such as the old and the new Parliament Houses in Canberra.

Jan's thimbles are signed 'Jan Milton' on the inner rim (*Plate 19*).

Lynn Richards

Lynn Richards was born in Hobart, Tasmania. She moved to New South Wales in 1965 and it was here that she commenced porcelain art lessons in 1979. She has had no formal training in art. Unhappy with the limited shapes of porcelain ready made for painting, Richards started making her own. After producing and selling small quantities of porcelain bisque she began experimenting with making her own moulds, concentrating on small items. She sold these blanks to other porcelain artists.

A love of detailed miniatures was emerging and it is not surprising that Lynn turned her hand to thimbles. In 1983 she moved to the Gold Coast in Queensland where she still lives. From 1990 onwards she stopped supplying blanks to other artists and concentrated on her own range of items, which includes brooches, vases and trinket boxes. She trades under the name of Lynn Richards Porcelain.

Richards' porcelain thimbles of cream and pink, with occasional forays into other pastel colours, are handpainted with flowers, with roses being her area of greatest expertise and the most popular design. The thimbles are embellished with 24 carat gold paint that sometimes includes the apex, and the resulting thimbles are very pleasing. Lynn's porcelain thimbles can undergo anything from three to seven firings depending on the type of decoration. Additional decoration can include raised paste and white scrollwork as well as gilding. She has currently added child's and miniature porcelain thimbles to her range.

Lynn marks her thimbles with 'Lynn Richards Australia' inside the rim. She also includes a personal numbering system which enables her to identify any product from her studio. This enables her to make matching sets of needlework-related items without needing to see the original piece again. This attention to detail reflects the meticulous skill of this highly regarded porcelain artist.

Lynn Richards of the Gold Coast's handpainted fuchsias

Russell and Creed

These two artists were commissioned exclusively by the Thimble Society of London to paint a series of thimbles. They were employed with a famous porcelain company in England. The series began in 1989 with two thimbles for each of the four seasons and after that new thimbles appeared quarterly. A series of Australian birds which includes the Australian Gouldian finch was part of this commission. The handpainting is by Master Painter Nigel Creed and the gilding is by Master Gilder Ken Russell. There are always two signatures on each thimble: 'Russell' is inside the thimble and 'NC' (for Creed) is on the outside. For illustration of the thimbles see the spring 1995 issue of *Thimble Society of London*.

Margaret Towler

Margaret Towler is a well known porcelain artist and respected teacher of porcelain art at Bluff Point in New South Wales. She is a graduate of the Teaching Institute of Porcelain Art NSW and a member of the Australian Porcelain Decorators Association. She enjoys the involvement of teaching and exhibiting her work, which includes thimbles, all over Australia. Thimbles are but a small part of her output.

The porcelain thimbles are made by Margaret's husband Bill Towler. Margaret's painted subjects are diverse and include original florals, birds, scenes and animals. The bisque porcelain thimbles may also have raised or incised decorative designs. She is currently working on thimbles with handpainted lace in the tradition of Irish Dresden thimbles. Once painted the thimbles are signed 'M Towler Australia' inside the rim. The thimbles are supplied with an explanatory card.

Judging from a survey conducted recently, Margaret's thimbles are widely represented in collections in Australia. Margaret has supplied Pan Arts with her handpainted thimbles which has ensured the widest possible distribution.

Margaret Towler of Buff Point's handpainted gum blossoms

Sylvia Tupper

Sylvia Tupper of Rosanna in Melbourne was commissioned by Beryl Warne of Thimble Collections in Melbourne to handpaint thimbles with roses and forget-me-nots for the opening of her shop in 1983. Tupper's fine handpainting also reveals her expertise with wildflowers. The thimbles are marked inside the rim 'Handpainted by Sylvia Tupper' and are supplied on a backing card with the artist's details.

Sylvia Tupper of Melbourne's handpainted bottlebrush

BREADDOUGH-ON-PORCELAIN THIMBLES

Breaddough is a form of decoration that was created from necessity during the Depression. It has regained popularity during the 1980s, especially in South Australia. Great dexterity is required for moulding tiny flowers, flower posies and figurines, which are affixed to thimbles. For breaddough to be successful it should not absorb moisture and must be treated properly so as not to attract cockroaches!

Caroline Cameron

Caroline Cameron was born in the United Kingdom and has lived in South Australia since she was 13. She started learning pottery but was looking to create something different. In 1985, once she discovered breaddough and was successful at making jewellery, she knew she had found a medium that she was happy working with. The breaddough that she uses is based on a recipe from the period between the World Wars, modified to include mould inhibitors and preservatives. Caroline produces breaddough figurines that sit atop unsigned, plain porcelain thimbles. Her inspiration comes from children's

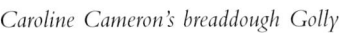

Caroline Cameron's breaddough Golly

storybooks and her mini figures include gollies, teddy bears, koalas (K11), fairies and elephants. These breaddough-on-porcelain thimbles are not signed.

Pan Arts have been Cameron's exclusive distributors since 1995 and to date she has supplied them with around 1250 thimbles, of which 200 have been channelled to The Thimble Guild in Scotland.

Judith Coombe, Kathryn and Jordana Thompson

Judith Coombe and Kathryn Thompson of South Australia teamed up in the early 1980s and created these fine breaddough posies on bisque porcelain thimbles. Kathryn began by making breaddough jewellery. The work has been continued by Kathryn's daughter Jordana, an architecture student whose artistic skills are evident in her breaddough creations. She has now perfected her craft to an art form. The breaddough is made from fresh white bread kneaded to a dough, to which is added special glues and non-toxic food colouring. The resulting colours are rich, not pastel. Each petal and leaf is hand modelled and attached to the thimbles and left to dry. They are then lacquered to seal them.

The thimbles are not signed. When only Judith and Kathryn were producing the breaddough, those thimbles came with a backing card, with the makers' details. Jordana has supplied Pan Arts with 500 of her breaddough thimbles for distribution around Australia; 170 of them have been sold to The Thimble Guild.

Breaddough-on-porcelain by Judith and Kathryn

POTTERY THIMBLES

Dorothy Andrews

Dot Andrews of Paris Creek Pottery in Meadows, South Australia, creates blank porcelain thimbles. Dorothy established her pottery in 1970 and her work is well known in South Australia. She colours the clay herself—the range of colours in her porcelain includes two shades of blue, yellow, pink, mauve, apricot, green, white, off-white and black. Dot's blank thimbles, left unglazed, have been used by countless painters and craftspeople throughout Australia. Dot also decorates her own porcelain thimbles with porcelain or Fimo flowers and has placed small frogs, ladybirds and handpainted miniature figures atop. On her blue and green porcelain thimbles Dot applies initials and monograms in gold. Some of her thimbles have tiny breaddough pale pastel flowers made by Marion Elliott attached.

Porcelain by Dot Andrews with breaddough by Marion Elliott

Tony Bouchet Ltd

Tony Bouchet of St Ouen in Jersey has perfected the making of agateware thimbles. Agateware pottery was first introduced to England about 1730 by Dr Thomas Wedgwood but discontinued in 1780. In 1963 Bouchet revived this method of pottery (a term used by Bouchet himself to describe his thimbles) and since 1984 has become renowned throughout the thimble world for his innovative thimbles for collectors. Agateware pottery involves staining white clay with metal oxides to give a marbled effect.

Bouchet's thimbles are entirely handcrafted. Their shape and texture is distinctive, in that they are taller than the average thimble and have a high gloss, smooth finish. The thimbles have a marbled or swirled effect to them and are finished with handpainted bands of 22 carat gold.

In 1987 Pan Arts commissioned Bouchet to make thimbles for Australia's Bicentenary. They are available in two colour combinations: yellow, with a green stripe flowing up and over the apex of the thimble, and in the reverse colouring: green with

Agateware by Tony Bouchet for Australia's Bicentenary

a yellow stripe. Both have the word 'Australia', a map of Australia and '1788-1988', all in gold, gold bands and gold circles on the domed, smooth apex. Bouchet included his backstamp in some of these thimbles while others have the Pan Arts backstamp inside. The thimbles are boxed (all the Bouchet thimbles are marked in the lid of the presentation box) and issued with a certificate of authority that includes the number of the thimble. The thimbles were limited in number to 1788. The thimbles were also made available to The Thimble Guild in December 1987.

Chelsea Girl Stoneware

Irene Barnett, who now lives in North Nowra in New South Wales, is the originator of Chelsea Girl Stoneware. Irene started making pottery in 1979 after being unsuccessful in finding a potter to make cream dishes or pots for the tearooms she and her husband ran at the Cambewarra Lookout in New South Wales. Through much trial and error learning Irene and her husband finally produced moulds for their stoneware products—tea and coffee pots, mugs, jugs and sugar bowls, items all allied to running the Lookout tearooms. This lead to creating their own souvenirs in stoneware and her fine white matt stoneware thimbles resulted. They are handpainted with kookaburras, blue wrens, waratahs, koalas and a few kangaroos, as well as the Kangaroo Valley Bridge and a map of Australia, and they all have 'Cambewarra Lookout NSW' printed on them. Irene made between 75 and 100 of these thimbles. Inside the thimbles are signed 'Irene Barnett Chelsea Girl Stoneware Australia Hand Painted'. When the Barnetts moved on about 1990, no further thimbles were produced.

Chelsea Girl Stoneware's kookaburra

Ian and Betty Lauder

The Lauders of Perth make handthrown pottery miniature thimbles and have being doing so since 1975. Ian and Betty arrived in Australia in 1984 from Whitby in Yorkshire. They had a pottery studio in England and when they retired to Perth, two of their seven kilns and several pottery wheels accompanied them.

The Lauders have specialised over the years in micro pottery—doll's house miniatures of 1/12th size. Neither has had the opportunity of attending pottery classes or had any tuition. Many of their techniques have been developed as they went along.

These mini thimbles are turned on the wheel by Ian, and Betty applies the decals and the gold trim. The thimbles range in height from 4 mm to 10 mm (about 3/16" to 3/8"). An amazing 1000 thimbles a year are produced, mainly for the miniatures market. The thimbles are unmarked.

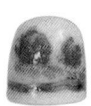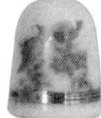

Ian Lauder of Perth's pottery miniatures range from 4 mm

Swagman Pottery

Swagman Pottery thimbles are made in Crestmead in Queensland. These brown monochrome pottery thimbles are decorated in relief in a dozen designs, all featuring Australiana—the echidna, emu, a homestead, kangaroo, koala (K12), kookaburra, platypus, possum, (merino) ram, a swagman and a wombat. The twelfth design, the Ettamogah Pub, can only be purchased at one of the pubs. There are no maker's marks.

Swagman by Swagman Pottery of Queensland

Christian Vocke

Christian Vocke is originally from Holland; he settled in South Australia and together with Ahmed Ptak of Auburn, also in South Australia, made moulded earthenware. This included mugs, plates, jugs, vases, bells, thimbles and ashtrays as souvenirs. In the 1980s Vocke slipcast ceramic thimbles and then handpainted Australian farmyard, Aboriginal and many varied South Australian scenes with low fluid glaze. Vocke's style is naive. The background colours are earthy, concentrating on the ochres, greens and browns, with the drawings in black contrast. Vocke also painted galahs and koalas in pinks and greys, and scenes typical of South Australia. These include various scenes of the copper mine at Moonta, the Whyalla steelworks and HMS *Buffalo* at Glenelg, in shades of ochre with the subject painted in black. Vocke was commissioned by Dorothy Andrews of Thimbella to make handpainted souvenir thimbles with town names on them which were distributed to various places in South Australia.

Though Vocke is no longer making thimbles, he is still producing pottery in the form of plates and bowls. His thimbles remain available through Thimbella, the primary outlet for his thimbles.

The thimbles are signed 'APCV or CVAP [their joint initials] Australia' and painted on the inside of each thimble. After Ahmed died the thimbles were signed 'CV Australia'.

Handpainted scenes of South Australia by Christian Vocke

Old Umbrella Shop

The Old Umbrella Shop in Launceston, Tasmania, built in the 1860s, has been operated by three generations of the Shott family. The shop is now preserved by the National Trust of Tasmania as a gift shop and information centre. The Old Umbrella Shop has had handpainted, cream coloured pottery thimbles made to advertise its wares. Three tiny coloured umbrellas are painted on them. Unfortunately there is nothing to identify the thimbles with The Old Umbrella Shop as there is no lettering anywhere on them—but they are a delightful thimble for collectors.

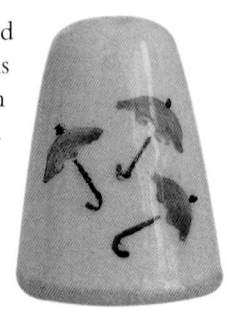

The Old Umbrella Shop Launceston

UNBRANDED CHINA THIMBLES

Firehydrant thimbles

Tourism is one of Australia's biggest earners. Unfortunately, Australian thimble makers have not kept up. Most of the thimbles available in tourist outlets are of poor quality.

The thimbles known affectionately as 'firehydrants' amongst thimble collectors worldwide are chunky china thimbles imported from Taiwan with plastic or metal discs or 'buttons' attached that stick out in a shape reminiscent of a firehydrant. The term was first used by collectors in South Africa in the mid eighties and has spread to countries where these thimbles abound. The 'buttons' are also found on teaspoons and souvenir stickpins. Collectors usually look for branded china thimbles bearing a backstamp and firehydrants have no markings.

Opals on firehydrants. Left: Coober Pedy; right: Lightning Ridge

There is an endless variety of firehydrants available. They make an excellent record of a trip or holiday, as they are found at every major tourist attraction and town across Australia, at a reasonable price (K13, K14, K15).

As well as appearing singly, firehydrants are available in boxed sets of six—these include

1 Gabler's Sydney Harbour Bridge enamel on silver thimble in original box

2 Pall Mall of Germany enamel badge on EPNS, showing the Sydney Harbour Bridge

3 German silver and enamel thimble

4 James Swann & Son's enamel on silver blue wrens

5 Ian Trafford-Walker's Indonesian-made gold on silver Byron Bay Lighthouse

6 Whitehill Silver & Plate Co enamel on silver budgerigars

7 *Palfrey's gold thimble*

8 *9 carat silver-lined Nifty*

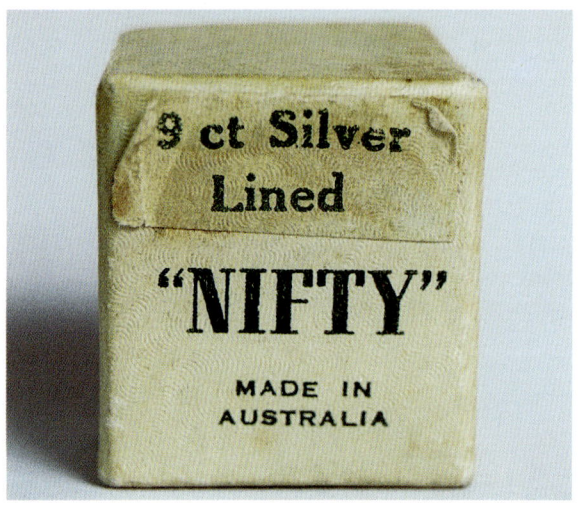

9 *9 carat silver-lined Nifty box*

10 *Price & Jardine's gold thimble with the New South Wales hallmarks for gold in 1927*

11 *Unmarked gold thimble thought to be made by Price & Jardine*

12 *PJP 9 carat gold thimble 1937*

13 *John Storm of Newcastle's gold and opal*

14 *Kyneton Fine China of Victoria handpainted by Rita Daniel*

15 *Royal Worcester's handpainted kookaburra 1929 with indentations in the sides*

16 *Royal Worcester's handpainted kookaburra 1926*

17 *Wedgwood's pink heath*

18 *Kookaburra handpainted by Gerald Delaney*

19 Jan Milton of South Australia's handpainted designs

22 Penfolds Wines with a black band

20 Boxed set of six Expo 88 Brisbane thimbles

23 Woodsetton Peep for Expo 88 Elizabeth Regina

21 Wear Ezywalkin' Boots (left) and Wear Ezywalkin Shoes (right)

24 Crummles enamel Sydney Opera House

China and Porcelain Thimbles

Set of six Melbourne scenes firehydrants

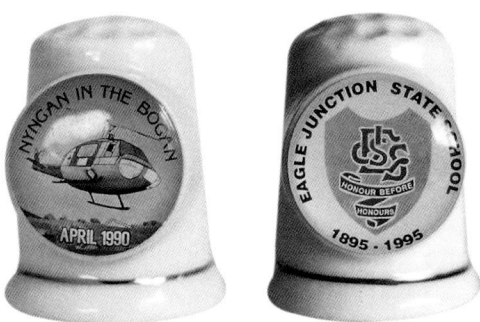

LEFT *Commemorating the Nyngan Floods in 1990*
RIGHT *Eagle Junction State School centenary 1895–1995*

Australian beers, scenes of Melbourne and Sydney, Australian birds, flowers, animals, Australian banknotes and so on.

Firehydrants are also used as fundraisers, e.g. by the CWA of Western Australia (Country Women's Association), the Blue Nurses of Queensland or the victims of the floods at Nyngan in New South Wales in 1990.

Schools are also using firehydrants as fundraisers or commemoratives, e.g. Eagle Junction State School 1895–1995 and Enoggera State School in Brisbane.

There are several firms producing this type of thimble in Australia; one is Nirex of Sydney, run by Don Clough; others are Chambers & Rowe Marketing and Goodwill Industries, both of Perth, and Emu Souvenirs.

Taiwan thimbles

Another range of Taiwan thimble blanks is imported into Australia where decals with Australian themes are applied. These again are large, chunky, poor quality thimbles but they abound in souvenir outlets all over the world. Made for specific outlets and tourist attractions, these thimbles usually appear in boxed sets of six; there are several multicoloured sets depicting Australian flora or fauna, and six different scenes of Melbourne in black monochrome. (See K16–K23).

Expo 88 was held in Brisbane for six months during 1988. Thimble collectors who visited the site early in the period were disappointed by the absence of Expo thimbles. In the last month, boxed sets of six Taiwan thimbles became available: it was a case of better these than nothing for collectors! It is not an easy commercial decision for thimble manufacturers and wholesalers to come to terms with, when these large franchisee events attract huge premiums for the use of their logo or symbol.

These commemorative boxed sets have six different decals; all have 'World Expo 88', and five of the six also have variations of Expo Oz the Platypus (*Plate 20*).

Taiwan blank thimbles have also been used by the Royal Flying Doctor Service as a fundraising exercise. For the diamond anniversary celebration in 1988, their commemorative thimbles had the RFDS logo in blue with the dates '1928–1988'.

The Australian Red Cross has also had fundraising thimbles made on Taiwan blanks that show the flag of Australia and a red cross superimposed over the map of Australia. Bold lettering for 'Red Cross' is on the verso.

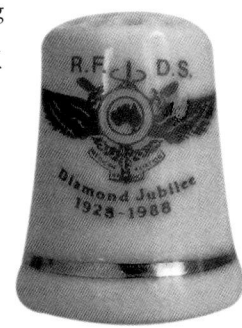

Diamond Jubilee of the Royal Flying Doctor Service 1988

There are few other unbranded china thimbles that are neither the firehydrant nor the Taiwan blank type, nor are they handpainted.

Snake Gully, the fictional home of Dad and Dave, Mum and Mabel, is famous on stage, screen and

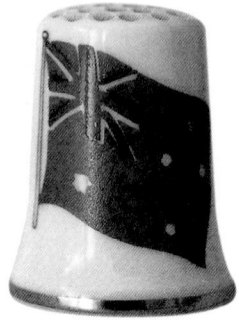

LEFT *'Snake Gully', the home of Dad and Dave*
RIGHT *Australian flag—made in Japan*

radio in Australia. Snake Gully thimbles are available showing the four characters in shades of green and red.

There are thimbles made in Japan with the Australian flag in colour as the design. The thimbles have a sticker inside that reads 'Limoges style Japan'.

The Harry Ramsden's chain are the world's largest fish and chips restaurants. The original shop was opened in Guiseley near Leeds in England in 1928. There are now branches around the world. The Melbourne outlet of Harry Ramsden's in Burwood East has china advertising thimbles available for sale. The thimbles have 'Harry Ramsden's' in bold red lettering across the front with 'The world's most famous fish & chips' in a circle around the name. The thimbles are only marked 'Fine English Bone China' on the inside rim.

Harry Ramsden's in Melbourne

In *The Thimble Collector* in 1986 Barbara Kelly brought to attention the Sydney visit of the aircraft carrier HMS *Illustrious* as part of the Australian Navy's 75th anniversary celebrations. One hundred china thimbles were aboard for sale to the visiting public. These had been produced by Bob Scott of Ipswich in England, a thimble dealer, whose son was in the British navy assigned to the *Illustrious*. None of these thimbles have been traced in Australia but they were all sold out during that visit.

Metal thimbles

Thimbles made in base metals, against those of silver and gold, are a twentieth century phenomenon as their production has become cheaper and cheaper; tens of millions have been manufactured for day-to-day sewing.

ALUMINIUM THIMBLES

Even though the aluminium advertising thimbles discussed below were made in Germany, Austria, England and the United States, they played a prominent part in giveaways in Australia prior to World War II. There are over 1500 products advertised on thimbles worldwide, but only a few are for products that are purely Australian. Many other thimbles advertised non-Australian products or services available in Australia, e.g. Singer Sewing Machines and Reckitt's Blue. To give some idea of the quantities produced, Aldridge (1985) indicates that half a million thimbles were made for Lyons Cakes alone!

All these thimbles were given away in Australia, as promotion, by suppliers with the purchase of items or in exchange for labels of the product being advertised. Some of the thimbles would have been supplied in bulk to shopkeepers to give out to customers. Grocery shopping was done by delivery or at the local grocers and it would have been easy to add in a thimble with the purchases. They were also found in show bags at the annual agricultural shows around the country, but no records exist of the contents of these bags. In Australia most thimbles were made for large national companies, e.g. Bushells Tea, so it is really exciting to find small or rural jewellers having aluminium thimbles made. Which other small concerns in Australia had these advertising thimbles made that have still to come to light?

A search through issues of *Australian Home Journal* from the twenties shows that though the companies which had advertising thimbles made did run advertisements, their thimble giveaways were not mentioned, other than the Bebarfald thimbles. It is amazing to find how many of the firms that commissioned advertising thimbles in Australia are still in existence today. Of the sixteen listed, nine are still trading!

These advertising thimbles were most prolific between the World Wars when the mass media was still in its infancy; they were a cheap form of advertising targeting the average housewife by giving her a useful gift.

These millions of aluminium advertising thimbles are all the same in shape and style. The product or service being advertised appears in raised lettering around the band. There is usually a star to denote the start or end of the slogan. The bands are painted in a variety of colours, leaving the lettering in relief plain to make it more legible. It is common to find that most of the paint has worn off with use, but scrapes of paint can still be found within the lettering to identify the original band colour. Examples have been recorded where attempts have been made to restore the band colour—this cannot be done very successfully.

Many of these thimbles have a coloured apex made of a type of plastic. Aluminium being such a soft metal, this reinforced top would give strength to the apex whilst sewing. These thimbles are generally referred to in thimble literature and catalogues as having 'glass' or 'stone' tops. The rims are generally rolled and some of these are in turn ridged.

The rest of the thimble is indented and so could be used for sewing. They were only made in one size. Because of the fragile nature of aluminium, many of these thimbles only exist today in a dented, out-of-round state; some even seem to have been used by teething babies!

On some aluminium thimbles, the country of origin is stamped into the band of the thimble, though it is usually found stamped in the indentations. Occasionally the country of manufacture is lettered up in the apex. It is interesting that most of the Australian advertising thimbles do have their country of origin stamped on them.

No aluminium advertising thimbles are currently being made in or for Australia, mainly owing to the high cost involved.

Charles Iles, one of the five largest thimble manufacturers in England, is known to have made aluminium advertising thimbles with coloured tops in the 1920s and 1930s in Birmingham. Ketcham and McDougall, thimble makers in America, made aluminium thimbles but there is no evidence that they produced advertising thimbles. In Germany advertising thimbles were made, amongst others, by Soergel & Stollmeyer and in Austria by Settmacher.

Though one cannot attribute any of the following thimbles to any specific maker, it is likely that Charles Iles made the Bebarfald–Blue Bird thimbles and some of the Bushells Tea thimbles, in which 'British made' appears up in the apex.

In 1993 D'Arcy Orders, a thimble collector in Portugal, compiled the most comprehensive list of aluminium advertising thimbles from around the world. Though the list is arranged by the subject advertised and it is not easy to trace individual brands, Australian products can be found scattered throughout.

The following Australian products are advertised on aluminium thimbles.

Allowrie Butter

The trademark Allowrie was registered for milk and other dairy products on 3 December 1932 for the Producers' Co-operative Distributing Society Ltd of Sydney. Allowrie Butter is still being produced in Australia today, by Bonlac

Allowrie Butter on a black band

Foods in Melbourne. The aluminium thimbles have a red or black band with the word 'Allowrie' in cursive lettering. The black band thimbles have 'Germany' in the indentations above the band. There is no coloured top to the thimbles.

Allowrie BUTTER ☆ [Germany]

'Assure in the A.M.P.'

The Australian Mutual Provident Society, founded in 1849, is one of Australia's leading insurance companies. Their advertising thimbles came with three different coloured bands: blue, dark blue and black. None of the examples found have coloured tops. The thimbles with the dark blue band also have the wording 'Made in USA' stamped in the indentations above the band.

Some of the A.M.P. thimbles have 'Made in Germany' lettered beneath the advertisement and the type of lettering is different.

Assure with the A.M.P. on a dark blue band (USA made)

ASSURE IN THE A.M.P. ☆ [MADE IN USA]

USA

ASSURE IN THE A.M.P. ☆ [MADE IN GERMANY]

Germany

Bebarfald–Blue Bird Sewing Machines

Bebarfalds were a chain of furniture shops operating around Australia from the 1920s to the 1960s. From 1922 onwards, amongst their range, they sold Blue Bird–Vickers treadle sewing machines imported from England. Special wooden sewing machine cabinets were commissioned by Bebarfalds in Sydney to house these machines. The cabinet features two leadlight panels on the doors and there is a blue bird in the glass in each door. Blue Bird sewing machines were sold throughout Australia in these and similar plain wooden cabinets. (Bebarfalds Corner in George Street, opposite the

  Metal Thimbles

Australian Home Journal, March 1, 1927.

FREE! Bluebird Thimble for the first 20 Coupons received.

More *frocks* for Less money!

the experience of thousands of women who own Bebarfald-VICKERS Sewing Machines

Women who own Bebarfald-VICKERS Sewing Machines, *get* the new dresses that they want; don't merely *wish* for them.

Bebarfalds have shown them a new, delightful, *picture* way to *make* them — underwear, dresses, coats, very modern and smart, for no more than the cost of materials.

Course in Dressmaking FREE! You can have them yourself if you select a Bebarfald-VICKERS Bureau Sewing Machine before March 31st, for Bebarfalds will give you a complete course of Picture Lessons in Dress-making entitled "The Better Dressmaker." free of charge. Bebarfalds fashion expert will tell you the style and colour of material that will suit you best.

Hemstitcher and Dressmaking Attachments FREE! So that you will be able to finish your frocks in the fashionable styles, you will be given 14 attachments for your sewing machine. With these you can hemstitch, shirr, tuck, pleat, ruffle and embroider automatically, more perfectly than by hand, and in one-tenth the time.

FREE Workbasket! Besides the *free* dressmaking attachments and free dressmaking course you will be given a roomy work-basket, which, when closed, makes an attractive occasional table.

No other firm than BEBARFALDS makes similar gifts or gives a similar service. Bebarfalds can only do so because they do not employ canvassers. These gifts are an extra inducement for you to buy direct, and not from door-to-door canvassers.

10/- Deposit secures this Gift Offer. The offer closes definitely on March 31st, but 10/- deposit paid now will secure it until you are ready to place your machine in your home. Send coupon for illustrated booklet and a FREE Blue Bird Thimble.

Bebarfald-VICKERS Bureau Sewing Machines.

Just a step in advance of the times! Guaranteed for your lifetime; *no risk* when you buy.

Sewing head made by Vickers Ltd., who built *the H M.S Renown*, on which the Duke and Duchess of York are coming to Australia. Made to match your furniture as a beautiful cabinet, with no ugly iron legs. You can use it also as a writing desk.

PRICES: from £9 10s. hand machines, to £22 18 6, or on extended term payments of 5/- per week. Not ordinary time payment, but this method is perfectly confidential because we employ no collectors.

We guarantee that the Bebarfald-VICKERS Sewing Machines will reach any address in Australia in perfect condition, because of our patent cork buffer packing method. We will refund your money if the Bebarfald-VICKERS is not exactly as we say. Let us send you full particulars. Send the coupon. There is no obligation.

Send for Free Booklet. The coupon will bring you a free booklet, illustrating Bebarfald-VICKERS Sewing Machines. Also a plan for saving money on your frocks. Send for this to-day. There is no obligation.

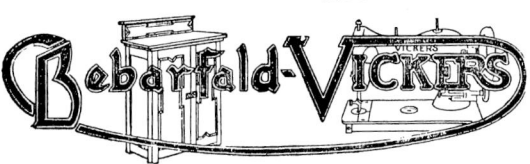

The Only Sewing Machine guaranteed for a Lifetime.
BEBARFALDS LIMITED, Opp. Town Hall, SYDNEY

COUPON — BEBARFALDS LIMITED, Opp. Town Hall, Sydney

Without obligation, please tell me how I can get more dresses for less money. Send me also your FREE illustrated sewing machine booklet.

NAME ....

ADDRESS ....

Make a cross here ☐ If you wish particulars of our monthly payment plan.

"H.J.", 1/3/27.

Send to Wertheim's, 440 Queen St. Brisbane, if you live in Brisbane, Maryborough, Toowoomba, Gympie or Ipswich. Wertheim's make an offer quite apart from *Bebarfalds*.

First advertisement mentioning the free Bebarfald-Blue Bird thimble giveaway

Town Hall, was a well known meeting place for friends in Sydney.)

Aluminium thimbles struck for Bebarfalds outlets in Sydney and Melbourne were given away between March 1927 and September 1940, according to contemporary issues of *Australian Home Journal*, where advertisements for the Blue Bird–Vickers Sewing Machines had appeared since April 1922. The initial advertisement read: 'Free Blue Bird thimble to the first 20 coupons received.' Later this was extended to the first 40 coupons and the thimble giveaways then were described as having a 'patent top'. This would mean that the thimbles with blue tops are later than those with plain tops. These are the only sewing-related advertising thimbles relevant to Australia.

'Bebarfald–Blue Bird Sewing Machine opp. Town Hall, Sydney' is lettered around the blue band, with the thimble having either a blue glass or a plain apex. Some of the Sydney Blue Bird thimbles have 'Made in England' inside the apex. Tubular needlecases in mottled Bakelite with 'Bebarfalds Ltd Opposite Town Hall George Street Sydney' were also produced as advertising material by Bebarfalds.

'Bebarfald–Blue Bird Sewing Machine 305 Lt Collins St Melbourne' thimbles also have a blue band and a blue glass top. Bebarfald's outlet in Melbourne only operated at this address between 1930 and 1932, so this is the easiest of the Australian advertising thimbles to date.

Bebarfald-Blue Bird Sewing Machines for Sydney (left) and Melbourne (right)

Boan Bros. Perth

Boan Bros., a chain of Western Australian department stores, was started in 1895. The name changed in 1917 to Boans. The firm was taken over and renamed in 1988 by Myer and, as Myer, still operates as department stores. The thimbles have 'Boan Bros Perth' lettered on what would have been dark blue bands with no coloured top. They would date from before 1917 when the company name first changed. There are no country marks of origin. These are the only known advertising thimbles for a large department store in Australia.

Boan Bros Perth

Bond's Hosiery

Bond's, of Camperdown in New South Wales, registered their trademark for hosiery and gloves on 5 January 1921. Bond's went on to produce socks and underwear but advertising thimbles were only made for their hosiery. The thimbles have a red band and no coloured top. The country of origin is Austria, which is stamped into the indentations.

Bond's Hosiery

'To see better see Mr B.'

Mr B the Optician was founded as the local optician in Perth in 1911 by Walter Buckeridge. Mr B the Optometrist still operates today as optometrists and contact lens practitioners in Perth, Busselton and Dunsborough in Western Australia, led by a fourth generation Buckeridge, John. The band on these thimbles is blue and there is a blue glass top with

Metal Thimbles

the advertising slogan reading 'To see better see Mr B'—surely most advanced marketing techniques for the time for a firm of opticians. It is unusual to find that these aluminium thimbles have crossed the Nullarbor into collections in the eastern states.

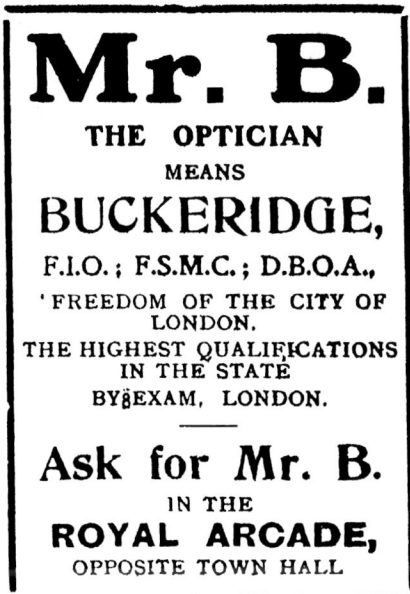

Mr. B. The Optician early advertisement (The Boomerang June 1919, courtesy Mr B the Optometrist)

'Burnet's Jellies for Purity and Flavour'

Holsum Products Pty Ltd of Rocklea near Brisbane were the trademark holders for Burnet's for jelly crystals from 3 December 1925, so their aluminium thimbles would date from then onwards. The Burnet's jellies thimbles have no coloured tops, and a red band with 'Made in Germany' is stamped into the indentations above the band.

Burnet's Jellies first started in Brisbane

Bushells Tea

Alfred T. Bushell first sold tea and coffee in Australia in Brisbane in 1883 and Bushells Tea remains a household name in Australia. Bushells were vigorous advertisers—*Australian Home Journal* in the 1920s carried different advertisements for Bushells almost every month. According to Bryden (1981) Bushells Teas spent £39,455 in 1923 on having free half-pound packets of Bushells Tea delivered to every home in Sydney. The trademark for the name Bushells was only taken out on 29 August 1935, by which time Bushells teas and coffees were household names. Bushells thimbles would have been found as giveaways in packets of teas. They would also have been exchanged for the labels from packets of tea; this vigorous marketing may be the reason that Bushells advertising thimbles are the most widely held advertising thimbles in Australian collections.

Bushells advertising thimbles were made in a variety of mediums: aluminium, Bakelite and brass, and the variety of slogans on the aluminium thimbles reflects the variety of teas available.

On first impression, the Bushells Tea aluminium thimbles appear to be all the same. The most commonly found thimble reads 'Bushells Blue Label Tea' around a blue band with a blue glass top. These thimbles have 'Austrian Make' stamped into the indentations. The thimbles with 'German Make' were made as the tops of sewing kits made for Bushells. A Bushells Blue Label Tea thimble was offered for sale in *Thimble Society of London* in autumn 1988.

From the left: Bushells Blue Label Tea (front); Bushells Tea of Flavour; Bushells Blue Label Tea (verso). Note the different shaped tops

Bushells – Tea of Flavour

The next most commonly found thimble has 'Bushells Tea of Flavour' on a blue band with a blue glass top. As can be seen from the photograph this particular slogan comes on thimbles of different shapes; one type has a smaller, more rounded apex than the other. The thimbles with the smaller rounded apex have 'British Made' lettered up in the apex. The others have no country of origin.

Less commonly found examples read 'Bushells Tea of Flavor' (the American spelling). These have a blue band, but no glass top. They are taller thimbles than those previously mentioned and there is no rolled rim or country of manufacture.

The thimbles with ' "Bushells" 1/3 Tea' are different from the other Bushells thimbles. Instead of the lettering being in relief, it is punched into the metal; the background band has fine vertical ribbing without colour and there is no coloured top. Does the '1/3' mean one-third of a pound in weight or one shilling and threepence? A search of Bushells advertisements of the 1920s and 1930s revealed no clues. There are no country of origin marks.

Bushells Tea of Flavor

Bushells 1/3 Tea

Bushells – Tea of Flavor

Bushells – 1/3 Tea

Cornwell's Malt Extract
Cornwell's sauces have been made in Australia since the 1930s. On 4 October 1938 Mauri Bros & Thomson (Aust) Pty Ltd of Canberra registered the name of Cornwell's for their malt extract. The thimbles have a plain top and the band is black. 'German Make' is printed on the band as part of the slogan.

Cornwell's Malt Extract

CORNWELL'S MALT EXTRACT GERMAN MAKE

Ezywalkin
Ezywalkin was first established in East Perth selling boots and shoes and Ezywalkin Pty Ltd registered the name of Ezywalkin on 1 August 1911. This shoe firm grew to have branches in Victoria from the 1920s until the late 1980s. There are two advertising slogans for Ezywalkin. The first have 'Wear Ezywalkin Boots' with a yellow band (a rare colour in advertising thimbles). There is no coloured glass top. 'German Make' is lettered below the band (*Plate 21*).

The second complements the first with 'Wear Ezywalkin Shoes'. These thimbles have red bands with red glass tops and 'German Make' is lettered in the indentations.

Wear EZYWALKIN BOOTS
GERMAN MAKE

German Make

Wear EZYWALKIN SHOES

'Grainus for Breakfast'
Grainus was an oat porridge. The trademark for Grainus was registered in November 1921 by Holsum Products Pty Ltd of Rocklea, near Brisbane. These advertising thimbles have a red band and no coloured top with no country of origin. See page 73 for lettering.

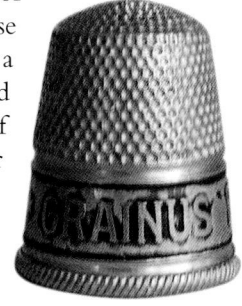

Grainus for Breakfast

25 Halcyon Days' Embroiderers Guild Victoria 1980

26 Halcyon Days' Embroiderers Guild of Western Australia 1980

27 Mark Models Bicentenary pewter thimble

28 Brass thimbleful for Hobart

29 Robert Herron's needlecase handpainted by Vicky Winters

30 Painted wooden top hat with silver Sydney Opera House and opal

32 John Trier's cattle horn and pewter

31 Col Ward thimbles. From left to right: lace flower tree, cypress 'Western Sand', athel tree and Webster's mallee

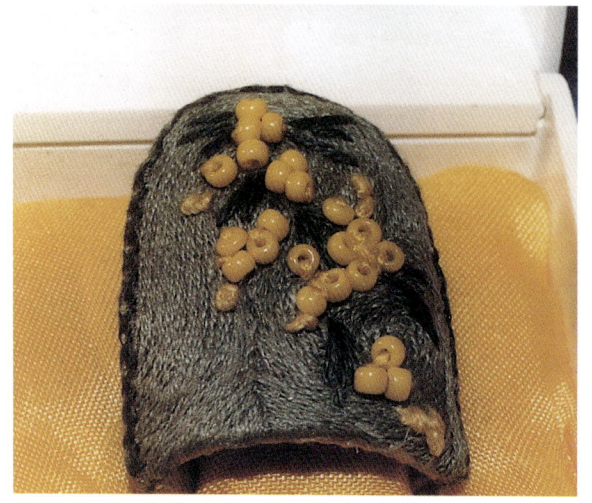

33 Embroidered silk and bead wattle thimble by Yvonne Winspear (Courtesy Yvonne Winspear)

34 Gumnut bush thimble

35 *Polymer resin by History Craft for Australia's Bicentenary*

36 *Nallyware plastic thimble issued during World War II to ADF*

37 *Eight sizes of Precision Plastics thimbles Sydney*

38 *Pilbara jade*

39 *Barossa Valley marble*

40 W. Dunkling Melbourne thimble box

42 Gunter's Melbourne

43 Anthony Hordern Sydney

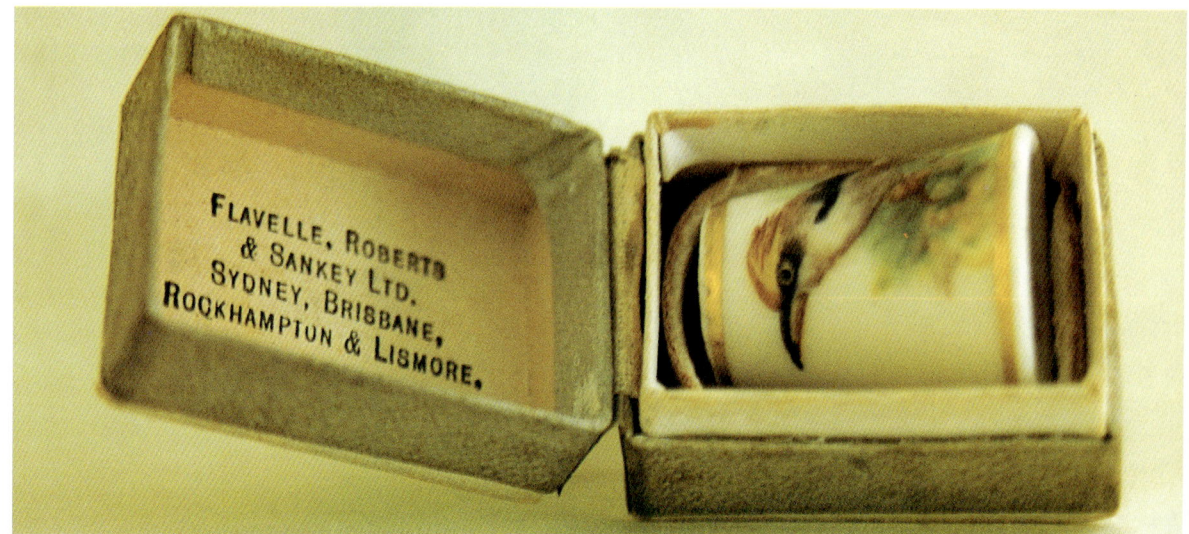

41 Flavelle, Roberts and Sankey of Sydney Brisbane Rockhampton & Lismore with Royal Worcester kookaburra thimble

Metal Thimbles

73

GRAINUS FOR BREAKFAST ✦

Penfolds Wines

Penfolds Wines were established in the 1860s in the Barossa Valley of South Australia by Dr Christopher and Mary Penfold; Penfolds are still flourishing winemakers today. The band is black and glass tops of yellow or black have been encountered, with 'Germany' lettered into the indentations (*Plate 22*).

PENFOLDS WINES ✦

'Use Pick-Me-Up Sauce'

The first advertisement for Pick-Me-Up Sauce appeared in *Australian Home Journal* in March 1920 and the sauce still appears on supermarket shelves today under the Cornwell's label. It was advertised as 'genuine Worcestershire Sauce made in Australia'. The thimbles have dark blue or red bands with the wording "Use Pick-Me-Up Sauce", no coloured tops and no marks of origin.

Use Pick-Me-Up Sauce

Early advertisement for Pick-Me-Up Sauce made in Australia (Courtesy Meadow Lea Foods)

"USE PICK-ME-UP SAUCE" ✦ ✦

ill.o66

J.J. Rafferty Chemist Armidale

J.J. Rafferty was registered as a chemist and druggist in New South Wales in 1898 and operated well into this century in Armidale. No colour remains on the thimble band on the examples sighted and no coloured tops; no place of origin is marked. It is most unusual to find thimbles made for a non-capital city in Australia.

J.J. Rafferty Chemist Armidale

J.J. RAFFERTY CHEMIST ARMIDALE ✦

'Silvafros for Stoves & Ironwork'

The Silvafros trademark was taken out by Taubmans Industries of Mary Street St Peters in Sydney on 23 June 1921 for their paint products. The first advertisement appeared shortly afterwards, in September 1921. Silvafros was a frosted silver enamel used to repaint kitchen wood stoves. Though Silvafros was advertised extensively in *Australian Home Journal* in the early 1920s, no mention of these thimbles was made. The thimbles sighted have no band colour remaining. As they were advertising a 'silver' product, maybe they never had any colour! They have no colour on their tops and no place of manufacture.

Silvafros for Stoves & Ironwork

SILVAFROS FOR STOVES & IRONWORK ✦

THIMBLES OF AUSTRALIA

LIKE FROSTED SILVER

"Every use of Silvafros suggests another."

The home uses of Silvafros as a protector and beautifier of metalware and woodwork are almost unlimited. Prepared from 99 per cent. pure Aluminium, Silvafros is easily applied and dries quickly with a silvery bright surface that not only pleases the eye but defies time, heat, rust and weather as well.

That "Frosted Silver" sheen which Silvafros imparts may be utilized in many novel ways. Bush flowers and ferns when coated with Silvafros make charming table decorations, retaining a "silver leaf" appearance for months. Use it on the Stove, Bath, Metal Pipes, Wire Mattresses, Motor Parts, Metal Gates and Fences and prove that—"Every use of Silvafros suggests another."

TAUBMANS LTD.
232 Castlereagh Street, Sydney.

SILVAFROS
Brilliant Aluminium Enamel

Australian Home Journal July 1923

F. & W. Stewart. Pty. Ltd. Jewellers

According to Cavill (1992), F. & W. Stewart have been jewellers in Launceston in Tasmania since 1879. Frederick and William Stewart established their business as 'watchmakers, manufacturing jewellers, electroplaters and gilders'. The business is still run by fourth generation Stewarts.

F. & W. Stewart Pty Ltd Jewellers

The thimbles have a dark blue band, with no coloured apex. There are no marks of the originating country on these thimbles.

F.&W. STEWART. Pty. Ltd. JEWELLERS

BRASS THIMBLES

Thimbles made of brass have been in existence since the fourteenth century, when Nuremburg in Germany was one of the pioneering thimble centres in the world. Millions of brass thimbles have been struck. They were the thimbles for day-to-day sewing until the twentieth century. Brass thimbles had the disadvantage of causing poisoning if verdigris (formed by the action of perspiration on the brass) entered the bloodstream. Brass is composed of two parts copper and one part zinc, giving it a yellowish colour.

'Bushells Rich Tea'

While many aluminium advertising thimbles have been made, brass advertising thimbles are much less common, so it is not surprising to find only one example advertising an Australian product. Brass advertising thimbles do not have coloured bands. This one has 'Bushells Rich Tea' lettered around the band. 'German Make' is stamped into the indentations but there are no other maker's marks.

Brass Bushells Rich Tea

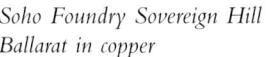

Bryan Fraser

Bryan Fraser of Artistry in Brass, Caringbah in New South Wales is known to have made brass thimbles but no examples could be located.

'Historic Berrima 1834'

Berrima is a town in the Central Highlands of New South Wales. Modern brass thimbles produced for Berrima have been lacquered green with a yellow band. They are lettered in gold with 'Historic Berrima 1834'. No other examples in this style for other Australian towns and cities have been located. There are no maker's marks.

Historic Berrima 1834 in brass

Soho Foundry

Soho Foundry at Sovereign Hill in Ballarat in Victoria is a recreated foundry where the metal spinners use old lathes. These are turned by a mass of pulleys and leather belts to make brass and copper pans, candle holders, domestic ware and thimbles.

The brass thimbles come in various sizes, the current ones being quite short. The wording 'Soho Foundry Sovereign Hill', around a mine headgear, is punched into the apex. These thimbles, made since the early 1980s, are still available for visitors to purchase at this recreated old mining village of the Victorian gold rush era of the 1850s.

Soho Foundry Sovereign Hill Ballarat in copper

Woodsetton Peeps

Woodsetton Peeps have been made in Dudley in England by David and Gill Bates since 1983. These thimbles have a peep set into their apex. By holding the outside of the apex to the eye, and looking towards the light, a small scene can be glimpsed. Victorian peeps, invented by Charles Stanhope, were made between 1860 and 1930; the scenes in those antique peeps can only be seen by looking into the thimbles.

Woodsetton Peeps are the modern equivalent of the early Stanhope peeps. It is possible to place a picture or peep, the size of a pinhead, into the apex of any modern thimble, be it of brass, pewter, wood, silver or china. Using patented lenses the picture is then magnified one hundred times. Woodsetton Peeps have a range of items with peeps, i.e. anything that can take a peep. If brass thimbles are used, they are usually lacquered and the thimbles are supplied in presentation boxes with an explanatory leaflet inside.

Woodsetton Peeps was commissioned by Pan Arts to put peeps into thimbles to commemorate Australia's Bicentenary in 1988. The result is brass thimbles lacquered in three colours: blue, green and red. They are otherwise identical, with 'Australia Bicentenary 1988' lettered on the front. The re-enactment of the First Fleet's voyage to Australia (May 1987–January 1988) is celebrated with a sketch of the *Bounty* and written details of the First Fleet inside the peep. Approximately 100 were

Bicentenary peep

Bicentennial Visit peep

produced in each colour. The design number (125) is part of the peep.

These thimbles were also for sale through the *Thimble Society of London* in their winter 1987 edition and *Thimble Collectors Guild* in January 1988.

During the Bicentennial celebrations in January 1988, Prince Charles and Diana made a Royal Visit to Australia. Peep thimbles were struck by Woodsetton Peeps to commemorate their visit. 'Prince of Wales' is lettered on these blue lacquered brass thimbles. Inside the peep there is a picture of the Royal couple with 'Prince & Princess of Wales Charles & Diana Australia Bicentenary 1988'. The design number (147) is in the peep.

As has been mentioned previously, there was a dearth of thimbles available to commemorate Expo 88. However, Woodsetton Peep thimbles were made for Expo—they are maroon lacquered brass thimbles with gilt bands and a rolled rim in gold. The thimbles have 'Elizabeth Regina' etched into the gold coloured band, so that on the surface there is nothing to link the thimbles with the Brisbane Expo. Peep inside! There is a sketch of HM Queen Elizabeth and HRH Prince Philip with 'Australia Visit' and 'Expo 88'. Elizabeth II opened Expo 88 in April of that year as one of the many ceremonies she performed during her Australian visit. The design number (148) is in the peep (*Plate 23*).

COPPER THIMBLES

Bryan Fraser

Bryan Fraser of Artistry in Brass, Caringbah in New South Wales, made copper thimbles before his death in 1995. He was a miniaturist who made thimbles in brass, copper and silver. Though not miniatures, his thimbles are not the full height of other thimbles. The example illustrated has a flower engraved on its apex and the sides are smooth.

Bryan Fraser's copper

Keith Warhurst

Copper thimbles were made in Hahndorf, South Australia, in the 1980s by Keith Warhurst, a metal spinner. The thimbles have a rolled rim and a hand indented apex, with smooth sides to the body. He made the thimbles for two copper mines, Burra in South Australia and Mt Isa in Queensland, and for Thimbella. Keith does several thimble shapes in spun copper. Burra Copper, which began mining copper in the 1850s, has been operating again in South Australia since 1971 and the copper Keith used comes from this mine.

Peter Hine worked with Keith—once Keith had made the copper thimbles, the indentations were made by hand and decals applied by Peter, who is also the distributor of the copper thimbles. The Burra thimbles have a decal of a map depicting Burra. Other Warhurst thimbles have decals with Gothic script monograms for the letters of the alphabet. Other decal designs include ladybirds, flowers and treble clefs.

Expo 88 peep

Copper by Keith Warhurst of Hahndorf

METAL THIMBLES

Soho Foundry
The Soho Foundry copper thimbles are identical to their brass thimbles (page 75). These thimbles are the only Australian thimbles to be included in Christina Bertrand's *Brass thimbles*.

ENAMEL THIMBLES
Other than enamel on silver thimbles, there are thimbles with enamel over brass and copper.

Crummles Enamels
Crummles Enamels of Poole in England revived an eighteenth century English method of painted enamels in 1974.

These delightful thimbles made by Crummles for the Sydney Opera House shop in the 1980s have an all round design showing scenes around the Opera House. The apex of gilt coloured brass has a fluted edge and fits the thimble like a cap. The lettering, 'Sydney Opera House Australia', runs across the front of the thimbles (*Plate 24*).

Crummles' thimbles never bear a maker's mark, but the boxes have the maker's details and an attractive explanatory leaflet.

Halcyon Days
Susan Benjamin opened Halcyon Days in Mayfair, London, in 1950, specialising in early enamel boxes. In 1968 she joined with Bilston & Battersea Enamels, a small family firm which made enamel objects, and these appeared from 1970. This partnership revived the Georgian art of fine enamelling over copper originated during Battersea's brief period of production between 1753 and 1756. This in turn had influenced Bilston's production of fine enamels between 1750 and 1840. The thimbles today are made by craftsmen; using ceramic lithography the designs are transferred to the enamel wich is then handpainted in Bilston in the Black Country.

In 1980 the Embroiderers Guild Victoria was looking for a quality item to celebrate their twentieth year since founding. It was appropriate that a thimble was chosen, as the founding of these guilds all over Australia in the 1960s had led to a resurgence of the use of the thimble for sewing. Halcyon Days was their final choice and these worthy thimbles were the result. The thimbles, enamel over copper with a neatly domed indented apex and a ribbed rolled brass rim, have a white enamel body. The main decoration is sprigs of Victorian pink heath with 'Victoria 1960–1980' lettered in green above. The Embroiderers Guild logo, a stylised pair of scissors, a thimble, two needles and threads, appears in green on the verso. A limited edition of 300 thimbles was ordered. This was the first of three commemorative thimbles ordered by the Guild in Victoria.

These thimbles bear the earlier (1970–1980) Halcyon Days backstamp that reads 'Halcyon Days' and 'Bilston and Battersea Enamels Made in England' (*Plate 25*).

In 1980 The Embroiderers Guild of Western Australia also commissioned a thimble from Halcyon Days Enamels to commemorate an anniversary of their founding in 1969. The State floral emblem of a kangaroo paw appears on a cream enamel background, with 'WA' above the flower. The apex and ridged rolled rim are of brass. The Embroiderers Guild's logo in blue is on the verso. There is no date on the outside of the thimbles but '1980' appears inside along with the small blue maker's backstamp for Halcyon Days, the newer of their two datestamps (1980–). These commemorative thimbles were supplied, with Halcyon Days Enamel's certificate of authority, in Halcyon Days cardboard boxes (*Plate 26*).

METAL THIMBLES

Australian Defence Force
The ADF issued 'housewives' (pronounced *hussifs*) to soldiers, sailors and airmen and women during World War II, which contained metal tailors' thimbles. The complete apex is missing in tailors' thimbles, as tailors use the side of the fingers for sewing. The thimbles are unmarked. Some of the thimbles are plastic but these have closed tops.

Alexander Gibson
Alexander Gibson of Rosebrook, Port Fairy in Victoria, applied for a provisional patent on 31 December 1915. The application number 18,302 related to 'improvements in and relating to thimbles'.

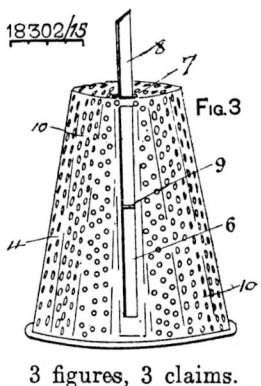

> **18,302.** 31 Dec. A. GIBSON, Victoria.
> **Class 42.1.**
> **Thread-cutting Thimble.**
> A thimble in which a small knife blade 8 is adapted to slide in and through the slots 6 and 7.
>
> 3 figures, 3 claims.

Preliminary sketch of Alexander Gibson's patented thimble (Australian Official Journal of Patents 8 November 1916)

This is listed in the *Australian Official Journal of Patents* for 1915. The provisional specifications were published on 3 November 1916 and the complete specifications accepted were advertised on 8 November 1916. Gibson then took out Patent No.103,548 in 1916 in Great Britain and was granted an American Patent, No.255,004, on 29 January 1918.

The patent was for a thimble with a thread cutter housed between the lining and the outer casing. According to the patent details and drawings, the cutter is a knife for cutting thread. There is a slot in the outer face of the thimble and the knife exits at the apex edge. The design shows an inner lining that protects the finger from any contact with the blade. There is a knob that slides the blade up and down the slot. The thimble is indented all over and there is a rolled rim. See Appendix 5 for the full text of the only Australian thimble patent (page 122).

No other details exist about this patented thimble, nor has an example been sighted. Alexander Gibson went to a considerable amount of trouble to register his patent in three countries but it is not certain whether the thimbles ever went into production or what they were to be made of. It is quite common that patented thimbles never reached production. Because this patent was granted during World War I, it may have been difficult to get the thimble into production.

There is an illustration and description of Gibson's thimble patent in Betensley, p.42, and it is also listed by Holmes (1990).

Yvonne Winspear

Yvonne Winspear of Sydney started collecting thimbles in 1983. After reading the trading columns in thimble catalogues from around the world, she decided to handcraft Australian thimbles to trade, as there were very few Australian thimbles available for purchase.

Winspear produced a whole range of thimbles between 1982 and 1988. The fourth design from this creative thimble collector/maker appeared in 1987, featuring string wound tightly around a metal thimble. Only 50 of these were made as they were very labour intensive.

String over metal by Yvonne Winspear of Sydney

PEWTER THIMBLES

Traditionally pewter has been known as 'poor man's silver'. Pewter is much softer and easier to mould than silver, but that also makes it an impractical medium to sew with. As a result the pewter thimbles of the later twentieth century have been made purely for the collectables market and are mainly novelty thimbles.

Buckingham Pewter

Buckingham Pewter Pty Ltd of Western Australia are producers of Australian-mined, fine quality pewter. Their range includes buckles, letter openers,

Geraldton wax by Buckingham Pewter of Perth

models, souvenirs, figures, coasters and plaques. In recent times they have diversified and included thimbles in their range. Pewter models are fixed to the top or the sides of sturdy thimbles turned in Australian timbers by Viv Paust. In some cases the timber is named and the thimble signed by the woodturner.

The pewter models included on the thimbles are Cooktown orchid, crocodile, dolphin, flannel flower, frill-necked lizard, Geraldton wax, gumnuts, koala (K24), kookaburra and swan. The thimbles themselves have no maker's marks for Buckingham Pewter, but each is supplied in a drawstring thimble bag with a card with the maker's details.

Exquisite Creations

Exquisite Creations is a British firm which makes pewter items. Sue Hopkins and Graham Parry of Victor Harbour, South Australia, were the Australian distributors for Exquisite pewter thimbles, bells and spoons, throughout the 1980s and into the 1990s. They commissioned the Australiana range of pewter thimbles.

The Australian Exquisite pewter thimbles mainly have the same cast base thimble: the word 'Australia' around the rim, with a bush scene of a gum tree, a map of Australia and a grass tree in relief around the thimbles. All the thimbles in the range have an item of Australiana atop—and some of these are in turn handpainted. There are no maker's marks on the thimbles, but the plastic presentation boxes are marked with the maker's name.

The Exquisite pewter range consists of:

Birds: Cockatoo, kookaburra, emu, pelican, galah, rosella, wedge-tailed eagle, magpie, fairy penguin, swan.

Australian icons: The Dog on the Tucker-box, merino ram, Sydney Harbour Bridge, dunny, horse tram, Cobb and Co, *Endeavour* (Captain Cook's ship), Ned Kelly, Sydney Opera House, Ayers Rock (Uluru).

Fauna: Echidna, frill-necked lizard, kangaroo, wombat, koala (K25), platypus, frog, dolphin.

Flowers: The flower range is only available handpainted: Cooktown orchid, golden wattle, kangaroo paw, Sturt's desert rose, waratah, pink heath, Sturt's desert pea, flowering blue gum, royal bluebell. These represent all the States' and Australia's floral emblems; each flower's name appears below it.

These thimbles were first imported into South Australia and there is also a range of South Australian designs depicting South Australian icons. The Australian Grand Prix was originally held in Adelaide and thimbles were made in 1985 to commemorate the event. The thimbles have a racing car atop (for racing enthusiasts some of the Grand Prix racing cars are handpainted in the various racing car colours).

The Barossa and Clare Valleys are world renowned for their wine; the thimbles for these areas have grapes on top. For collectors of ships the Exquisite range includes several early ships of significance to South Australia: *One and All* (a sailing ship), HMS *Buffalo* (these thimbles were commissioned for the 150th anniversary of the founding of South Australia); *Falie* (ship). The wombat for South Australia's 150th Jubilee in 1986 and the Old Gum Tree at Glenelg complete the range.

In 1994, Pan Arts took over from Sue Hopkins as distributors for Exquisite Creations. Pan Arts have continued to handle existing designs and are extending the range.

LEFT *Cobb and Co. by Exquisite Pewter*
RIGHT *South Australia's 150th anniversary by Exquisite Pewter*

Firehydrants

Though firehydrants are generally made of china, a small proportion are made of metal or pewter. The pewter thimbles have an extruded part that holds a plastic shield. Many of the thimbles are marked 'Made in Japan' up in the apex. As with their china counterparts, these sturdy metal thimbles may be found in tourist outlets throughout Australia with a variety of scenes (K26).

Australian flag—pewter made in Japan

Fort Pewter

Fort in the USA used to make pewter thimbles. They are Florida based and have made a range of Australiana thimbles. The thimbles are quite functional, unlike many other pewter thimbles, with the top half of the thimble being indented and separated with a ridge from the plain band. The rim is rolled, with indents. It is the apex that identifies the thimbles as Fort thimbles. It is flat with a fluted edge with the principal decoration sitting flat on it. Examples of a kangaroo, a koala (K27) and a kookaburra in relief in the apex have been found in collections in Australia. These may have been part of a series of Australian fauna. Though these thimbles are not marked with any Fort maker's marks, not many of their American theme thimbles were marked either.

Kangaroo by Fort Pewter

Stephen Frost Warwick Models

Stephen Frost of Warwick in England is one of the world's top pewter miniaturists. Warwick Models Ltd was established in 1981 by Stephen, after having been with Macmillan & Wife as a pewter thimble model maker. Gallery One Thimbles are the Australian distributors for Steve's range of thimbles and his Australiana thimbles were commissioned by them during the 1980s.

The range includes a koala (K28), the Sydney Opera House, a platypus and a kangaroo—fixed either to the side or the top of the thimble. They are of plain pewter. A map of Australia is on the body of the thimbles, with the rest having a beaten surface.

Frost is best known for his thimbles where miniature characters form the thimble. The bust of the character is the body of the thimble; a feature of these thimbles is that the hat is usually hinged. His fully painted range includes Aussie Shearer thimbles, some complete with corks around the hat.

Steve's thimbles are stamped 'SF Warwick Models' inside.

LEFT *Sydney Opera House by Stephen Frost*
RIGHT *The Aussie Shearer by Stephen Frost*

Mark Models

Trevor Power of Mark Models Ltd in Birmingham has made thimbles for Pan Arts. As preparations to celebrate Australia's Bicentenary began, Dick and Ann Wallace looked for Australian pewter manufacturers to make commemorative thimbles. On drawing a blank, Mark Models was commissioned. The resulting Bicentenary thimbles, in pewter and bronze coated pewter, were cast with the map of the world in relief, with Australia highlighted in red on the bronze pewter and in gold on the plain pewter thimbles. The design also contains a sailing ship and an aeroplane to depict the two hundred years of Australia's progress. The lettering around the rim has 'Advance Australia 1788–1988'. The apex has 'Ltd Edition No.../5000 pieces'. Though limited to 5000 numbered thimbles, only 3000 were taken up by Pan Arts. The thimbles are boxed with a small tag reading 'To commemorate the arrival of the First Fleet . . .' (Plate 27).

Two hundred and fifty of these thimbles were supplied to The Thimble Guild in 1987 for their mail-order business, thus ensuring their widest possible distribution.

Apex of Mark Model Bicentenary thimble

METAL THIMBLES

Mark Models also made a kangaroo and a koala (K29) atop thimbles available in gold or silver-plated pewter. The thimbles are engraved erroneously on the inside rim with 'Pan Arts Melbourne'. This has led to some confusion amongst thimble collectors, as Pan Arts have only ever been based in Sydney.

Miniature Kingdom Collectables

In 1989 Gallery One commissioned Miniature Kingdom in Devon, England, to design thimbles with a koala in pewter on top of a bone china thimble. The handcast koalas are finely moulded and handpainted. Early editions of the koala thimble have the backstamp 'Miniature Kingdom Fine Bone China'. Current issues have 'Fine Bone China Made In England' as the only marking in the thimble. The thimbles are accompanied by an explanatory leaflet. Some of these koala thimbles have been marketed in the United States through Gimbels of Maine in their annual mail order catalogues (K30).

Moorland Miniatures

Moorland Miniatures of Devon in England make pewter thimbles. In 1995 they added a kangaroo to their range. The pewter kangaroo with a joey in the pouch sits atop a thimble decorated incongruously with acorns and oak leaves in relief around the sides. There are no maker's marks on the thimbles.

Kangaroo by Moorland Miniatures

Pan Arts

Pan Arts finally located a firm in Sydney in 1989 to make Australian pewter thimbles. These thimbles, made by Ray between 1989 and 1991, are intended for the tourist market, not for use. The original seven designs of large sized thimbles, first cast by Ray, are in pewter. Around 1400 thimbles were produced during this period. The thimbles are usually not marked; if they are, the words 'Pan Arts Sydney ©' are crudely scratched on the inside rim.

PAN ARTS SYDNEY ©

Mark inside the apex

New moulds were made in England from the original silver masters made in Sydney and these proved more satisfactory. Michael took over casting of the Pan Arts pewter thimbles in 1992 in Sydney and to date nearly 2800 thimbles have been made. Michael is Russian born and he arrived in Australia to start a new life in the late 1970s. He was creating items for the fashion industry—buttons, buckles, and so on—when his path crossed that of Pan Arts, who persuaded him to make thimbles. The thimbles made since 1992 are much finer and neater in appearance. These 'new' pewter thimbles are now stamped in the apex with 'Pan Arts Australia Made' though some may still have the name roughly scratched in as well.

There is a map of Australia in relief on the apex of each thimble and the current range has been expanded to eleven designs in relief on the sides. These are the Sydney Opera House; 'Christmas Downunder' (three designs): a surfing koala, a bush party with the fauna all wearing Christmas hats, and harbour boating; Australian fauna; Australian flora; Australian owls; 'Corroboree' (dancing Aboriginal figures and a didgeridoo); a koala in a tree, 'Waltzing Matilda', with the words of this famous Australian tune in relief; and 'Waltzing Matilda' with the Jolly Swagman. The thimbles each have lettering on the verso, describing the scene. Michael's thimbles for Pan Arts are also available as brass, silver and gold plated pewter (K28, K31).

Sydney Opera House in pewter for Pan Arts

P G Enterprises

P G Enterprises of Yorkshire in England made pewter thimbles for consignment to Gallery One in 1992. The thimbles have a flying kangaroo, similar to the QANTAS symbol, on the top, and the apex has been indented. Alternating bunches of wattle, gumnuts and acorns appear in relief around the thimbles. There are no maker's marks. These thimbles are not currently being produced.

Kangaroo by P G Enterprises

Riccardo's Pewter

Pursuing her idea of getting more Australian thimbles available for trading with thimble collectors overseas, Yvonne Winspear persuaded Riccardo Pipimenle of Sydney to make thimbles in the late 1980s. Riccardo is a well known pewter worker in Australia, turning out quality pewter goods. There was much experimentation before Yvonne and Riccardo were satisfied with the results.

Riccardo's pewter thimbles are available with various Australian fauna or the waratah fixed to the side of the completely indented thimble. 'Australia' is engraved above the rim. Being cast, the thimbles are heavy and quite thick walled. There is an engine-turned striped decoration to the rolled rim.

His range includes the kookaburra, echidna, platypus, wombat, koala (K32) and the New South Wales waratah flower. Today Riccardo leaves the apex smooth and highly polished and 'Australia' is not lettered on the thimbles. Riccardo's thimbles have no maker's marks.

Opals fixed to the body of pewter thimbles have also been a very popular design from Riccardo. His thimbles are still available at The Rocks in Sydney.

Marylyn Verstraeten

Marylyn Verstraeten has pewter thimbles (K33) made in the same mould as her silver thimbles (page 40).

Other pewter thimbles

Some of the most unusual Australian thimbles struck in pewter are those in the shape of a fruiting banksia cone. Banksias grow all over Australia but the *Banksia grandis*, found in Western Australia, produces the woody cones represented on these thimbles. There are no maker's marks and no further details are available.

Pewter banksia cone

Other pewter thimbles with Australian themes have been marketed by Gimbels, a mail order concern in Maine (USA), notably those with kangaroos and koalas. The American makers are unknown and some of the likenesses are not very accurate. The relevant Gimbels catalogues are dated 1981, 1991, 1992 and 1994.

SILVER-PLATED THIMBLES

Perfection Plate

Perfection Plate Holdings Pty Ltd are situated in Revesby in Sydney and have been making heavy quality silver-plated Australian thimbles with a 'button' in the apex for the souvenir market since the late 1980s. The body of the thimbles is vertically

LEFT *Waratah by Riccardo's Pewter*
RIGHT *Echidna by Riccardo*

ridged and the multicoloured 'buttons' are similar in type to those found on firehydrant china thimbles. There is a heavy rolled rim to the thimbles and no maker's marks.

The thimbles are presented in bubble type plastic packaging where details of the manufacturer may be found.

Perfection Plate silver-plated design

Portuguese thimbles

Modern Portuguese silver and silver-plated thimbles are well known amongst thimble collectors worldwide. The hub of Portuguese thimble making is centred on Oporto in northern Portugal and Topazio are the most renowned thimble makers. The lightweight thimbles with their distinctive shape, with a flat apex and intricate embossing, are easily recognisable. These Portuguese thimbles are made in two parts: the body of the thimble is first cut to shape from a sheet of silver-plate, the decoration die-stamped onto this flat shape before the thimble is rolled together and soldered. Then a circular disc, cut to form the apex, is indented and soldered to the circular tube to complete the thimble.

One of these Portuguese thimble designs with an Australian connection is of silver-plated brass with a small enamel Australian flag attached to the front of the thimble. There is a waffle pattern on the top third of the thimble. The verso is ornately embossed with acanthus leaves and tiny flowers. The rolled rim is striated. The inside of the thimble is gilt coloured, where the embossed design is clearly visible. There are no maker's marks, but there is a distinctive four-pointed star or medallion in a circle on the apex, which is only lightly indented. This four-pointed star is the mark of Topazio for their silver-plated brass thimbles. These thimbles were made during the 1970s and 1980s.

Australian flag from Portugal

The Australian flag thimble is one of several designs made for the world market with flags of different countries.

THIMBLEFULS

Tot measures or spirit jiggers, in the shape of very large thimbles, are known as 'thimblefuls'. They are exact replicas of thimbles, including the indentations. On average they measure about 50 mm (2") in height. They were made for the souvenir market.

Each thimbleful has a metal or enamel badge attached to represent various tourist attractions or towns. They have existed in Australia since the 1960s.

Iles & Gomms would have made the most commonly found thimblefuls, those made of chromed metal. Iles & Gomms of Birmingham were the world's biggest producers of functional thimbles in the twentieth century until they ceased production in 1990. Other thimblefuls were made of brass (*Plate 28*) or were silver-plated. Some would have been handmade. The rims are not commonly rolled, but examples do exist with rolled rims.

The lettering varies from thimbleful to thimbleful: the Iles & Gomms thimblefuls have 'Just a Thimbleful' lettered across the top of the thimbles, when the thimbles are placed on the apex, with the open end upwards. Others read 'Thimbleful' or 'Thimble Full'. Some have no lettering at all.

Towns and attractions in Australia for which thimblefuls are made include Canberra A.C.T.,

Chrome thimbleful for Railway Station Townsville

Casino, Gundagai, Hobart, Kempsey NSW, Kosciusko, New Norfolk Tasmania, Orange NSW, Tamworth, Townsville Railway Station, Western Australia.

Thimblefuls are also available in wood, made by Robert Herron of Tasmania. His thimblefuls are of Huon pine, with 'Just a Thimbleful' pyrographed onto them.

Handmade silver-plated thimbleful for Kempsey

Robert Herron's wooden thimbleful

Wooden thimbles

There are thousands of woodturners in Australia, with almost as many types of timber to turn. Lovers of our indigenous wood should consider a specialised collection of thimbles from as many Australian timbers as possible. Woodturners are encouraged to include the name of the timber used inside the thimble, and their name or initials.

Listed here are the better known or more prolific thimble turners. Also included are wooden thimbles that have been handpainted. A further listing of woodturners turning thimbles in Australia appears in Appendix 3 (page 115).

David Appleby
David Appleby of Newcastle in New South Wales was a Master Woodturner. Encouraged by Barbara Kelly, who was the outlet for his thimbles, David used a wide variety of Australian timbers to create his range of sturdy thimbles. In 1988 one of Appleby's wooden thimbles was presented to Queen Elizabeth II during her visit to Newcastle for the Bicentenary celebrations. He died before it was presented to the Queen.

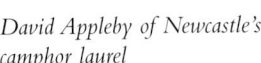

David Appleby of Newcastle's camphor laurel

Doug Birrell
Doug Birrell will be familiar to thimble collectors in Australia as the editor of the *Needlework Tool Collectors Society of Australia Newsletter*. Doug came to needlework tools through his interest in wood turning and carving. He is very aware that wooden thimbles have not to be crudely proportioned, poorly sanded or coated in heavy gloss finish to catch the eye of the collector or tourist. His wooden thimbles rather reflect the skill of his turning with fine attention to detail. Doug has perfected his art in the form of inlaying and laminating different woods; he has realised that the design possibilities in thimbles are enormous. He uses different coloured Australian timbers and incorporates laminated contrasting colour timbers of various shapes and design. Each thimble is different. The thimble illustrated is from 'The Eye' series, which is made of sycamore and inlaid with rosewood, black bean and bamboo. With so many timbers used in one thimble, Doug supplies an explanatory note with each one.

Doug Birrell's inlaid 'eye' design

Ruth Floth
Ruth Floth has used finely turned thimbles and hand decorated them in a folk art style. She is known for her handpainted teddy bear designs. Her thimbles are signed 'Ruth Floth' inside.

Ruth Floth's handpainted wood

Lyn Foster
Lyn Foster is an internationally recognised folk artist who lives in Newcastle, New South Wales. There she runs the Foster Folk Art Studio teaching her craft; she also takes classes in Sydney and lectures and teaches overseas. Foster has published books on

Handpainted folk design by Lyn Foster

folk art painting. Lyn has handpainted wooden thimbles in her distinctive folk art style, decorating both the body of the thimble and the apex. The thimbles are unsigned.

Margaret Handley

Margaret Handley commissioned some finely turned wooden thimbles that were good enough to handpaint using her skill as a doll artist. Her finely executed roses on an all-over painted background will do any thimble collection proud. The apex and the inside of the thimbles are painted gold. The thimbles are not signed.

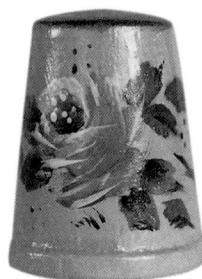

Handpainted wood by Margaret Handley

Robert Herron

Robert Herron of Riverside in Tasmania has been a woodworker by trade since 1963. He realised in 1980 that interest in thimbles was growing worldwide, particularly in thimbles made from local Tasmanian timbers. His association with Australian thimbles has spanned nearly two decades. Herron's thimbles are instantly recognisable as they are all turned to the same dimensions and shape and he has remained a popular source of innovative collectables.

Timbers used in his thimbles vary from the rich yellow Huon pine endemic to Tasmania and rapidly becoming rare, through to the rich browns of blackwood, the pinks of myrtle and the variegations of sassafras. These variations are highlighted in his laminated timber thimbles. Some of the timbers he uses are rainforest species. The thimbles are turned and finished to show the natural beauty of these special timbers.

Each of Herron's thimbles bears a sticky label with details of the timber used and 'Made in Tasmania'. His current thimbles include his business name (R.& K. Herron) and the address or phone number.

Herron also makes a range of novelty thimbles. These include a tiny Huon pine mouse with leather ears and tail attached to a blackwood thimble. Very Australian are the Convict thimbles, where Robert has taken a plain Huon pine thimble and affixed a tiny black ball and chain to the rim. They are finished with the convict arrow pyrographed on both sides (1993). There are also eucalypt wood thimbles with tiny gumnuts attached, and thimbles with a mini wooden apple and pear affixed. Other thimbles in Robert's range are his 'one cent coin' thimbles, where a resin-coated coin is set into the apex, with the possum side of the coin visible. (One cent coins are no longer legal tender in Australia.)

LEFT *Robert Herron's Huon pine convict design*
RIGHT *Robert Herron's horizontal wood*

There is also a series using five historical timbers. The first is of horizontal wood; the bark of this timber clings to the wood even when the thimbles are being turned. The others are made of Burmese teak from an old Tasmanian railway coach, the Windermere oak, camphor laurel and Huon pine. All these thimbles are supplied with a leaflet detailing the origin of the timber from which they are made.

Open-ended tailors' thimbles in Tasmanian woods are another product from Herron.

Laminated timber by Robert Herron

Herron has also created popular 'grandmother/granddaughter' thimble sets. As the name suggests, they are pairs of thimbles of differing sizes in matching timbers.

Similar to Robert Herron's laminated thimbles are his multi-timbered thimbles made of about one hundred pieces in five timbers: blackwood, eucalypt, myrtle, celery top pine and Huon pine. The thimbles are accompanied by an explanatory leaflet.

In 1991 his first needleholders, of Huon pine, had blackwood thimbles as the top.

Thimblefuls by Robert Herron are also available. See the section on Thimblefuls (page 83).

For Australia's Bicentenary in 1988, Herron produced wooden handpainted thimbles with a sprig of wattle inside a map of Australia and the dates '1788–1988'. Robert himself painted these designs. Robert has also handpainted some thimbles with Tasmanian devils, small and aggressive carnivorous marsupials found only in Tasmania.

Herron's wooden thimbles are so finely turned that many artists have been moved to embellish them with their own designs. Some of Herron's thimbles, up until 1990, were handpainted by former Tasmanian Dianne Williams, whose expertise is painting wildflowers. She painted the thimbles with the flowers of the timbers they were made from. Nowadays thimbles are handpainted by Robert's daughter Joanna Wigzell with brightly coloured native Australian animals and birds—the kookaburra, rosella parrot, scarlet robin, wombat, possum and echidna. Joanna's portrayal of the blue wren is especially popular. Each thimble bears the name of the bird or animal portrayed. They are not signed.

Other sets of Herron thimbles have been pyrographed by Frea Pecheur. Robert commissioned Frea, but not many of these sets were produced. The plain wood is a fine backdrop for the Australian fauna Pecheur has intricately 'drawn' in pokerwork. The set of eight includes: echidna, feathertail possum, kangaroo, koala (K34), platypus, sugar glider, wallaby and wombat. Each has 'Frea Pecheur' burned into the inside.

Vicky Winters of Sydney won an art competition when she handpainted a shoe with the traditional painting of her ancestors. Commissioned by Barbara Kelly, Vicky used Herron's wooden thimbles and needlecases for her rich handpainted Aboriginal designs that completely cover the thimbles. These traditional designs from the Dreamtime incorporate figures and animals in the dot style of painting. No two thimbles are alike. They are the only thimbles handpainted by an Aboriginal artist. Winters painted approximately 30-40 of these designs. The thimbles are not signed. Vicky has also handpainted a small number of Herron's needlecases, where there is a larger surface to display her talents as an artist (*Plate 29*).

Dorothy Andrews of Thimbella has fixed finely moulded breaddough posies of coloured flowers to Herron's plain wooden thimbles.

Robert Herron makes thimbles to special commission, including thimbles for the Patina Craft Gallery in Echuca with a paddle boat painted on them, and of the Sydney Opera House for a stallholder at the markets in The Rocks in Sydney.

Nancye Crooks, a collector from Victoria, was instrumental in getting sets of six of Herron's thimbles

LEFT Robert Herron's Bicentennial design
RIGHT Handpainted rosella on Robert Herron thimble

LEFT Pyrographed possum on Robert Herron thimble
RIGHT Vicky Winter's Aboriginal painting

for sale in August 1989 through The Thimble Guild, bringing native timbers of Australia to the wider collecting community. Unfortunately the thimbles were so highly priced that her purpose would have been defeated. Robert has recently sent a consignment of his Australian thimbles to Gimbels mail order house in the United States, which should ensure further exposure for this talented Australian craftsman.

Bob Malacari

In 1990 the Embroiderers Guild of WA celebrated their 21st birthday. To commemorate the event Bob Malacari, a woodturner in Perth, was commissioned to turn thimbles of various Western Australian timbers. The thimbles are presented on backing cards with blue lettering with the commemorative details, including the Embroiderers Guild logo. The names of the timbers used are written on the back of the folded presentation cards, and the thimbles are also marked with the maker's name, the timber and 'Western Australia' on the inside of each thimble.

Commemorative for Embroiderers Guild of WA by Bob Malacari 1990

Sandra Menger

Sandra of Brisbane has been practising the art of pyrography (pokerwork or wood burning) for 17 years. In 1991 Sandra published *Pyrography: the art of creative woodburning,* which established her reputation as one of Australia's finest pyrographists. The many faces of the Australian animals that Sandra sketches on wood are created with lifelike expressions.

Since 1996, Sandra has used her skills to burn the tiniest floral designs on Col Ward's plain wooden thimbles. Sandra also creates sets of thimbles which are set atop wooden pegs on wooden plinths in the shape of Australia. Her current designs include sets of six wildflowers, each showing fine detail, and sets of seven dunnies, an 'Australian institution'.

Pyrographed gumnut by Sandra Menger

Sandra Menger's set of seven pyrographed 'Aussie dunnies'

Needlework Tools Collectors Society of Australia

The first Corroboree (conference) was held in 1990 in Malvern in Melbourne for members of the Needlework Tool Collectors Society of Australia. This first conference was a milestone for thimble collectors in Australia and Huon pine thimbles were commissioned from The Deeping Woodturner in Tasmania to commemorate the event. Handpainting by Fiona Curry with a wattle and bottlebrush design finishes off the thimbles. The thimbles are neatly domed and finely indented on the apex and are signed 'FC'. 'Corroboree 90' is lettered

Corroboree 90 for Needlework Tool Collectors Society of Australia

around the rim. The thimbles are available in two sizes—one regular and one child size. Only 130 of these thimbles were made.

Pan Arts

Pan Arts, in pursuing their quest for Australian thimbles, have discovered several woodturners who between them have made thousands of wooden thimbles. Many of these thimbles are left natural but many others have been adorned or handpainted.

Mervyn Kennedy is a hobbyist woodturner in northern New South Wales. With his love and understanding of timber he was commissioned by Pan Arts in 1992 to make wooden thimbles that were then painted black. Opal triplets were set into the apex. Mervyn made 350 of these thimbles for Pan Arts. A quantity of them was supplied to The Thimble Guild.

Keith Adams of Port Macquarie in New South Wales is a woodturner who has produced wooden thimbles for Pan Arts in the shape of a top hat. These thimbles have a black gloss painted finish and a silver decoration of a tiny three-dimensional Sydney Opera House (made and attached by Peter Grossman of Sydney). Some of these silver castings have an opal incorporated in the design (*Plate 30*). Keith also turns other thimble hat shapes in plain timber, as well as good quality Australian timber thimbles and thimbles in the shape of Christmas bells, an Australian wildflower. The latter are handpainted.

Bob and Margaret Greschke are a team producing fine quality handpainted wooden thimbles. Born in Germany, Bob settled in Australia, and initially farmed. Now he makes fine staircases in Melbourne. Bob is also a woodturner and has supplied 2000 wooden thimbles to Pan Arts. Margaret has handpainted an additional 1100 wooden thimbles featuring a range of different designs including include Aborigines in tribal dress, koalas (K35), blue wrens, waratahs, kangaroos and farm scenes; these have sold successfully throughout Australia and to The Thimble Guild.

Margaret has also painted custom orders for The Thimble Guild, including 100 thimbles for 'Christmas 1993' and a special edition, solely for them, the 'Ashes 1993' cricket series. These thimbles are turned from recycled willow wood and have 'Winners 4-1 Australia' painted on the verso. Her

Handpainted scenes by Margaret Greschke

thimbles are simply signed 'MG' on the outside. Bob has also produced 140 'thimble nests' from a variety of Australian timbers, three thimbles fitting one inside the other.

Peter Grossman, silversmith and pewter caster, makes pewter attachments and affixes them to Bob Greschke's wooden thimbles for Pan Arts. His range of pewter castings include Australian birds and animals (K36).

Handpainted 'Ashes 1993' by Margaret Greschke

Olga Stack

Olga Stack was enterprising enough to place an advertisement for her folk art in Kalgoorlie Airport. Her handpainted thimbles are similar in style to Margaret Handley's with an all-over handpainted background with flowers such as roses or pansies handpainted on them. She also handpaints needlecases and darning eggs that she purchases from South Australia as wooden blanks. Her thimbles are signed on the inside rim plus the date. Olga now resides in Perth.

Handpainted pansies by Olga Stack of Perth

Malcolm Walter

Malcolm Walter, the highly regarded silversmith from Stirling in South Australia, has turned to using wooden thimbles as a medium for his silver and other metalwork, including pewter. His gumnuts, koalas, rural scenes, Aboriginal designs, ringtailed possums, butterflies—all designs first created for his fine quality jewellery—are fixed onto wooden thimbles. The silver motifs are marked in the same manner as his sterling silver thimbles, with 925, 'MW' conjoined, and a hopping kangaroo each in a lozenge stamped into the silver.

Silver possum by Malcolm Walter

Col Ward

Col Ward of Mansfield in Brisbane was looking for a new interest before he retired. Being passionate about the different timbers of Australia Col was searching for a medium to utilise his hobby of wood collecting. Joyce Nixon-Smith, a thimble collector in Queensland, suggested that he make wooden thimbles. When Col Ward turned his first wooden thimble in 1991, based on examples Joyce had given him, he never dreamt that he would accumulate such a vast collection of beautiful timbers in the shape of thimbles. Col's approach to thimbles is different from other collectors. He is not interested in thimbles for functional use, rather he's a collector presenting his collection of timbers as wooden thimbles.

To date he has turned over 3000 thimbles from more than 650 timbers. The shape of his thimbles is determined by the grain and he uses 110 shapes to do this. The thimbles are lacquered to enhance the grain and all his thimbles are turned to the same internal diameter. Through his membership of the International Wood Collectors Society Col actively seeks out pieces of timber that will reflect the beauty of the grain in each of his wooden thimbles (Plate 31).

Col Ward has also sought out historic timbers and created a story using the thimbles and the original pieces of wood to tell a story. One example is the Mataranka Homestead in the Northern Territory, which has been recreated in miniature, with accompanying thimbles turned from timber found on the property.

Col will happily turn thimbles to size for anyone interested in having wooden thimbles to use; he makes blank thimbles for Sandra Menger to pyrograph and for his wife Beryl to handpaint with violets or Australian wildflowers and abstract designs.

Yvonne Winspear

Yvonne Winspear has handmade several innovative types of thimble over the years. The third design to come to fruition, in 1986, was a paperbark thimble. Paperbark is a cork-like substance from the tea-tree or melaleuca in New South Wales. Paperbark is moulded over wooden thimbles of Tasmanian leatherwood which Yvonne obtained from a woodturner in West Gosford, New South Wales. Yvonne handpainted Aboriginal stick people, with spears in hand, in black around the thimbles, which are signed 'YW' on the bark. A matt finish Estapol preserves the thimbles. Yvonne made about 600 of these thimbles, some were marketed through the Thimble Collectors Guild in January 1987. In 1988 in Spokane, Washington, at the Thimble Collectors International (TCI) Convention, Yvonne's bark thimble won 2nd prize in the Wooden Thimble section of the Artisans' Competition.

Winspear's most recent thimbles, wood with a cream chamois covering, were made to celebrate the Bicentenary of Australia in 1988. These chamois thimbles have a sailing ship handpainted on the front, with '1788-1988' and stick figures representing the Aborigines on the verso. The thimbles are signed 'YW' on the chamois. The flat apex is covered in tiny black beads. One hundred and twenty thimbles of this design were made and 100 were sold in July 1987 through the Thimble Collectors Guild.

All Yvonne's thimbles have a gold sticker map of Australia inside.

LEFT *Yvonne Winspear's handpainted paperbark*
RIGHT *Yvonne Winspear's chamois design for the Bicentenary*

Other thimbles

Some of the thimbles in this section have been made as novelties and are not intended for use, rather being produced for the collectables market. There are some great skills required in making these thimbles, some produced by master craftspeople. Collectors are often keen to obtain thimbles of as many different materials as possible and here Australia has not lagged behind.

CRYSTAL AND GLASS THIMBLES

The glass-blowers who hold demonstrations of glass-blowing in shopping centres around Australia can often be persuaded to blow thimbles. There will be many examples of these one-off creations.

German crystal

These sets of six crystal thimbles with crystal birds atop, including the sulphur-crested cockatoo, are made in Germany. The birds are frosted and perch on top of hexagonal-shaped crystal thimbles. The thimbles are unmarked but the presentation boxes are marked 'Fingerhut Tannenzapfen' and 'Crystal colours'.

Sulphur-crested cockatoo crystal from Germany

Malcolm Walter

Malcolm Walter obtains lead crystal Ullmannglass thimbles through Pan Arts and adds his own silver motifs to them. Principally a jeweller, Malcolm's motifs are created from his silver jewellery and fixed around the German crystal thimbles. The motifs are gum leaves and gumnuts; koala (K37); Sydney Opera House and Harbour Bridge; a rural farm scene incorporating a windmill and rainwater tank; kangaroos and the Aboriginal Dreamtime, incorporating the dot effect on a snake, kangaroo and turtle. The crystal thimbles are vertically ridged inside and smooth on the outside; the effect of these 'silver crowns' on crystal is very pleasing. 925 and 'MW' are stamped into the silver designs, along with a hopping kangaroo, the same maker's marks as on Walter's sterling silver thimbles (page 41).

Pan Arts are the distributors for Malcolm Walter's thimbles. Walter has produced over 1000 of these thimbles to date, with about one-third being supplied to The Thimble Guild, ensuring the widest possible distribution of these fine Australian/German thimbles.

Malcolm Walter's silver design of Sydney Opera House and the Harbour Bridge over crystal

HORN AND BONE THIMBLES

Allan Davis

Allan Davis of Bellerive in Tasmania made whalebone thimbles, thimble holders and needlecases during the 1980s. These needlework accessories are made from one-hundred year old whalebone found in Tasmania at an early whaling station. Allan supplied these thimbles to Thimble Collections in Melbourne in the early 1980s. The thimbles have been left

100-year old whalebone by Allan Davis of Bellerive

unadorned with a raised ring turned in the body of the thimbles. There are no maker's marks.

John Trier

John Trier was born in England and in 1948, at the age of sixteen, came to Australia with his family. Having worked with cattle and sheep all his adult life, he started working with cattle horn in 1977. John is a self-taught artist and he began by making horn buttons, then salt and pepper shakers, scarf rings, crochet hooks and lace bobbins, all by hand carving.

In late 1979 Joyce Nixon-Smith saw John Trier's work in craft shops and asked him if he would make thimbles. He has since handcrafted hundreds of thimbles and supplied craft shops throughout Australia as well as collectors in the USA. The apex has a criss-crossed pattern. In 1980 he added scrimshaw of Australian animals—bandicoot, echidna, kangaroo, koala (K38), platypus, possum, wombat—and also made open-topped thimbles similar to tailors' thimbles. His range included other needlework related items—crochet hooks and tatting shuttles. The thimbles were supplied with a small label inside identifying the thimble maker.

John's Tamrookum Valley Craft is situated near Beaudesert in south-east Queensland. In 1986, on his retirement, John began the Associate Diploma in Jewellery and Silversmithing. Initially he combined horn and silver but soon switched to pewter, finding this metal more sympathetic to horn. He received a 1995 Churchill Fellowship, enabling him to pursue his study of cattle horn work overseas.

John stopped creating handmade horn thimbles in the early 1990s but continued making fine cattle horn collectables and exclusive pewter and horn jewellery. His work is found in galleries around Australia.

In 1997 John was convinced by Sue Gowan that his thimbles are still sought after and he has started to produce thimbles again.

Scrimshaw on cattle horn by John Trier of Beaudesert

His new range of horn thimbles reflects the sophistication and beauty he brings to his modern cattle horn work. His thimbles are no longer handmade but turned, and the beauty of the turned cattle horn gleams with the polished surface. The apex is of highly polished pewter, with indentations. Plain horn thimbles are to become available again but John is no longer applying scrimshaw to his thimbles (*Plate 32*).

IVORY THIMBLES

By the 1950s Albany in Western Australia was one of Australia's last remaining whaling stations, so it is not surprising to find that most Australian ivory thimbles are made from old ivory from the area.

Ralph Bennett

Ralph Bennett of Albany has handturned small dainty thimbles out of sperm whale ivory. They are completely unadorned, with a flat or slightly concave apex. There are rings incised in the apex and there is a rim to the thimbles. The full beauty of the ivory is shown as these thimbles have been polished to a fine sheen, reminiscent of mother-of-pearl. There are no maker's marks but a card accompanying the thimbles gives the maker's name and address. The thimbles were made in the 1980s.

Ralph Bennett of Albany's whale ivory

James Cumberland-Brown

James is renowned for his scrimshaw. He acquired a great quantity of sperm whale ivory from the old whaling station in Albany before the sale of whale ivory was banned in 1972. This miniaturist, from the Royal School of Fine Arts, has created exquisitely scrimshawed thimbles.

As a scrimshander, James was made an Associate of London's Royal Society of Miniature Painters, Sculptors and Engravers. When membership is limited to sixty members worldwide, one realises the honour bestowed on this skilled craftsman. This membership entitles him to exhibit annually at the Royal Society in London.

OTHER THIMBLES

Scrimshaw by James Cumberland-Brown of East Fremantle

His thimbles show scrimshaw of sailing ships, figures, country scenes, lighthouses, abstract flowers, acorns with oak leaves and abstract patterns. The scenes are carved with a probe or sharpened nail, with black oil paint rubbed into the carvings to bring them to life. The thimbles are signed 'JFC' and are supplied with a certificate proclaiming 'This is to certify that this tooth was taken off the West Australian Coast prior to 1972'.

James turns the ivory thimbles himself and the shape varies from thimble to thimble. He is also known for his wooden thimbles. Originally residing in York, Western Australia, where visitors to Hillside could watch the artist at work, he now lives in East Fremantle. The thimbles are still available from the artist (K39).

LEATHER THIMBLES

R. Reidler

Leather thimbles are favoured by quilters as they are kind on the fingers and have a reinforced padded tip to give the extra strength needed whilst quilting. These thimbles are partly open-topped, allowing the finger to 'breathe' whilst sewing; being so soft they have been known to have been sewn to a quilt! These thimbles are handmade in South Australia by R. Reidler. There are no maker's marks.

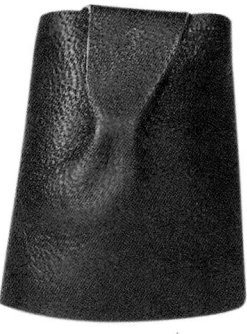

Leather quilter's thimble by R. Reidler

Yvonne Winspear

In March 1983 Yvonne created her first kangaroo skin thimbles. They are Asian in shape (like the silk Kolmi thimbles from Korea) and 45 mm (1¾") in height. The furry side of the leather is on the outside. Colours vary from light beige to dark brown. A small quantity was made from the pure white fur that comes from the belly of the animal. The thimbles are decorated with gold-plated kangaroo stickpins. The first thimbles were offered for sale in the *Bower Bird Magazine* in Brisbane. Yvonne handmade approximately 700 kangaroo skin thimbles, an amazing feat. To export these thimbles, which she did extensively (Kay Sullivan of De Vingerhoed in the Netherlands offered Yvonne's thimbles for sale in 1985), Yvonne had to have the permission of Australia's National Parks and Wildlife Service.

White curly-woolled sheepskin was Yvonne's second design. The thimbles are made in the same shape as the kangaroo skin ones and are of the same height. The stickpins are in the shape of a map of Australia. These were sold through a newspaper advertisement in Australia and through a shop in The Rocks in Sydney. Approximately 100 were made.

LEFT *Kangaroo skin by Yvonne Winspear*
RIGHT *Sheepskin by Yvonne Winspear*

For other thimbles by Yvonne see the Metal and Wooden thimble sections (pages 78 and 90). A hobby that started with necessity as the mother of invention turned into financial reward, as 1500 thimbles have been made for the American, Scottish, Australian (through The Thimble Collector) and Dutch mail order thimble markets.

None of Yvonne's thimbles is currently being produced.

Yvonne Winspear (Courtesy Y. Winspear)

NATURAL FIBRE THIMBLES

These novelty thimbles have been created for trading with other thimble collectors. Crocheting, tatting and knitting are skills allied to sewing, embroidery and quilting and it is a natural progression to turn a hand to creating thimbles with cotton or woollen thread. These thimbles have to be stiffened with sugar water to retain their shape. All have been produced more as a challenge than in great quantities.

Crochet

Betty Duschke and Barbara Martin of Perth crocheted thimbles with fine cotton thread.

Crochet by Betty Dutschke

Embroidery

In 1986 Yvonne Winspear made a one-off, never-to-be-repeated thimble. Handstitched and embroidered, it is made entirely of green silk stitches and decorated with tiny yellow beads and French knots signifying wattle, the national flower of Australia. This special thimble won 1st prize at the 1988 TCI Convention in Spokane in the Exotic Section. It also won 2nd prize in the Artisans Section at the South African Thimble Convention in 1990 (*Plate 33*).

Knitting

These thimbles were knitted using hand-spun Australian wool by Barbara Martin of Perth. The thimbles are hat-shaped and made in natural brown or white wool colours.

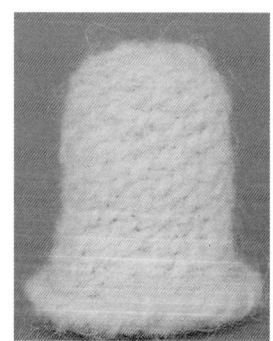

Knitting by Barbara Martin

Lace

Elena Dickson of Queens-land is a knotted lace expert. Using a needle she has knotted finely textured lace thimbles. A backing of stiffened board helps the thimbles retain their shape and acts as a background to the fine work.

Knotted lace by Elena Dickson

String

Thimbles were made in small quantities by Barbara Martin of Perth using tie-dyed string. Once it was dyed, the string was sewn together to form thimbles.

Tatting

Margaret Hickling of Kilcoy in Queensland, Kay Collins of Brisbane and Barbara Martin of Perth have all experimented successfully with finely tatted thimbles.

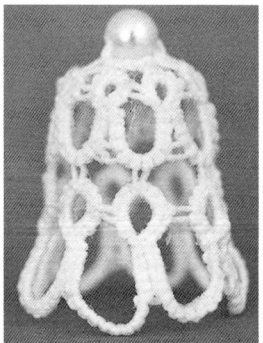

Tatting by Margaret Hickling

PAPIER-MÂCHÉ THIMBLES

Haley

The late Hal Bennett from Apollo Bay in Victoria created his first papier-mâché thimble as a surprise for his wife Shirley in 1979. The Bennetts had recently returned from a visit to Kashmir where all the world's papier-mâché thimbles were made; this first thimble that he made for Shirley led to the development of a cottage industry by these two enterprising Victorians.

After the success of the first thimble Hal, an instrument maker, refined his process until he had a marketable commodity. There were five stages to the making of his papier-mâché thimbles. He reduced paper to pulp, then added other ingredients (whiting, linseed oil, Aquadhere glue and oil of cloves) to make the papier-mâché. From this mixture the thimbles were shaped by hand, sandpapered smoothly, undercoated and finally coated with a clear varnish.

The Bennetts went to Buckleys in Melbourne with their first dozen papier-mâché thimbles. When there was a repeat order, the enterprise was born. In 1979 Haley papier-mâché thimbles were sold throughout Australia and to thimble outlets overseas. Ruth Baum of London advertised the Haley thimbles for the first time in May 1981 in her *Shopping Service* mail order thimble catalogue. *Thimble Society of London* was another of the overseas outlets the Bennetts supplied: the advertisement for Haley thimbles appeared in their autumn 1982 issue. The trading name Haley was a combination of the names *Hal* and *Shirley*.

There are five papier-mâché thimble designs: Australiana, floral, opal tops, Australian postage stamps, and Haley-Glo (the thimble that glows in the dark). Shirley, a talented artist, who together with Hal had been in advertising, did all the art work and handpainted the thimbles. A feature of Shirley's thimble artwork is the hand decorated apex. The backgrounds come in a variety of colours.

The thimbles are smooth with no indentations. They all have a sticky label inside identifying the thimbles as 'Haley Hand Made Papier-Mâché'. A few bear Shirley's initials, 'SB'. Many of the thimbles have the word 'Australia' painted around the rim and have the year they were made on them. A novel idea on many of the thimbles was an Australian opal set into the apex.

The shape of the Haley papier-mâché thimbles is quite distinctive; if the sticky label is missing, they can still easily be identified by their shape.

Some Haley thimbles were made for the Australian Collectors Club. They have a bower bird, the club's symbol, painted in black on the front, on a yellow-orange base, and are signed 'SB' with the date '1984' painted on the apex.

Another design incorporates used Australian stamps to form a collage over the papier-mâché—these were made in 1982 as the stamps used date from this time.

The fauna painted by Shirley includes kangaroo, platypus and koala, and several Aboriginal scenes exist (K38, K40).

Only one example exists of the Haley-Glo, the thimble that glows in the dark. This experimental thimble never went into production.

The Haley thimbles were made over a period of six years—through ill health Hal was forced to give up making thimbles in 1985.

Papier-mâché by Haley of Apollo Bay

PLANT MATERIAL THIMBLES

A number of novelty thimbles have been created from plant material by talented thimble collectors looking to supplement their collections and having handmade thimbles to trade.

Gumnut thimbles

Gumnuts from the eucalyptus tree are mainly associated with Australia, although gum trees are now grown in several other countries where the climate is similar. Some of the larger gumnuts are naturally thimble-shaped and it was only a matter of time before they appeared as thimbles. This kind of thimble is called a 'bushman's thimble'. The eucalypts growing in Western Australia tend to produce the large kind of honkynuts needed to make thimbles, so it is not surprising to find this example from Kalbarri in Western Australia with

'Kalflora, Kalbarri' on the attached plastic badge. There are no further maker's marks (*Plate 34*).

Monstera deliciosa thimbles

Barbara Martin used the dried calyxes of the *Monstera deliciosa* plant to weave and stitch these novel thimbles, finished with a bow of the same fibre.

Monstera deliciosa

Tagua or corozo nut (vegetable ivory) thimbles

Vegetable ivory, from the nuts of the palm genus *Phytelephas* of South America, was used to make needlework tools and thimble cases in Victorian times. These items are highly prized today amongst needlework tool collectors. The nuts were easy to carve and some of the decoration on these tools is intricate. Vegetable ivory darkens with age from a creamy to a honey colour; animal ivory does not.

Those who have worked with tagua or corozo nuts, which are naturally full of irregular holes, will realise how difficult it is to turn a thimble from a tagua nut.

Ray Brittain of Brisbane, who began to experiment with tagua nuts in 1996, has had some success in turning thimbles from this material. They are beautiful to handle, as their smoothness is their dominant feature. Ray's thimbles have 'RB' and 'Tagua nut' written inside them.

Jim Clarke of Perth, a wood turner and wooden thimble maker for years, rose to the challenge of making tagua nut thimbles in 1992. The caramel colour of Jim's thimbles, which inside still have the rich brown colour found in some tagua nuts, are the work of a skilled turner. Jim has not marked his tagua thimbles.

PLASTIC THIMBLES

According to DerMarderosian (1986), it is very difficult without a chemical analysis to determine the composition of any given plastic. Plastics in the form of celluloid first appeared in the second half of the nineteenth century and were known as Xylonite. Ivorine thimbles, made by Charles Iles from 1913, would also fall into this category. By adding various fillers to plastic, a great variety of colours from pastels through to mottled, tortoiseshell and pearl lustres result.

Bakelite

Bakelite was the trade name of the General Bakelite Company; this early plastic was patented in the USA in 1909 by Leo H. Baekeland. Thimbles of Bakelite were produced roughly between 1914 and the 1950s. It is unusual to find Australian advertisements on Bakelite thimbles but two kinds have come to light.

Bushells Tea had advertising thimbles made in Bakelite in the 1920s to complement their range of aluminium and brass advertising thimbles. These thimbles are of a distinctive dark blue Bakelite and have the lettering 'Bushells Blue Label Tea' in white around the band. There are no marks of origin on the thimbles. Unlike their aluminium counterparts, these Bushells thimbles were produced in different sizes. Very few examples still exist of these Bushells Tea thimbles, leading one to speculate that only a few (100?) were ordered—maybe as giveaways for more important clients.

The second kind are cream coloured Bakelite thimbles advertising Orchard's Watches of Sydney. R. B. Orchard the watchmaker, situated on the

Bakelite Bushells Blue Label Tea

Tagua nut thimbles. Left: Jim Clarke; right: Ray Brittain

OTHER THIMBLES

corner of King and Pitt Streets, was the forerunner of Prouds, longstanding Sydney jewellers. Orchard's slogan in the 1920s was a catchy 'Orchards where the best watches grow'. The thimbles are completely plain, with the lettering 'Orchard's Watches' (not in colour) around the band. There are no other markings.

Bakelite Orchard's Watches of Sydney

ORCHARD'S WATCHES

Ray Brittain

In 1996 Ray Brittain of Brisbane started to turn thimbles. Having mastered wooden thimbles, Ray sought something different. His novel thimbles are made of a synthetic material. From a multicoloured stick of plastic, Ray turns these unusual thimbles—the colours ranging from striking tiger's eye to opal to marble—all in synthetic plastic.

The thimbles are straight sided and smooth and the apex is indented with rings. Because of the highly patterned polished surface the thimbles have no maker's marks.

Synthetic material by Ray Brittain

History Craft

Resin thimbles have been variously marketed throughout the world as reconstituted or replica bone, ivory dust or sweepings, simulated horn, plastic or resin. Resin thimbles are devised to look and feel like ivory without the stigma that ivory attracts. Resin thimbles are manufactured in Cirencester in England, by a small studio called History Craft to recreate the beauty of nineteenth century scrimshaw. They call them 'polymer ivory'.

In 1988, Pan Arts commissioned through Macmillan and Wife another design for Australia's Bicentenary, this time from History Craft. These creamy coloured thimbles have the ship *Young Endeavour* etched on them to look like scrimshaw and '1787–1788'. On the verso is a scroll lettered with 'To commemorate the voyage of the first British settlers... 18th January 1788'. There is a miniature metal compass under perspex in the apex, and there are no maker's marks (*Plate 35*).

Approximately 100 thimbles were made. Thimble Collectors Guild marketed some of them in June 1987.

Marquis and Nally Ware Plastic

These two firms manufactured plastic picnic ware (mugs and plates) and yoyos, amongst other things, in Sydney in the first half of the twentieth century. The marks on their Nally picnic ware are 'Royal Nally Ware Made in Australia'. Nally still operates in New South Wales making plastic ware—nowadays they make recycling bins.

Nally also made thimbles, in the period leading up to World War II. They are different from the Precision Plastics thimbles (see below), in that they are very mottled in appearance and have no maker's marks on them. They were produced in many sizes, including larger sizes for men, and in a large range of darkly mottled colours, corresponding to the other products in their range at the time. The size numbers appear up inside the apex.

These cheap thimbles were produced for the school sewing room and were sometimes given away with other sewing items. There are thimbles by Nally Plastic in the army issues of 'housewives' in World War II (*Plate 36*).

Needlework Tool Collectors Society of Australia

The second Corroboree of this Society was held in Melbourne in 1992; these thimbles were amongst the giveaways to Conference delegates. 'Made in the USA' is lettered up in the apex. The thimbles are of white plastic and lettered in bright blue with 'Needlework Tool

Plastic Needlework Tool Collectors Society of Australia

Collectors Society of Australia' around the band. Two hundred and fifty thimbles were commissioned through Bob Hum of San Diego.

New Zealand

New Zealand has manufactured chromed plastic thimbles, in a similar shape to those made by Perfection Plate Holdings in Australia (page 82). These thimbles are very lightweight, and have vertical ribbing down the body, with multicoloured 'buttons' in the apex portraying many of the tourist attractions around Australia. The thimbles are marked 'New Zealand Made' up inside the apex.

New Zealand chromed plastic

Personalised thimbles

In the United States personalised plastic thimbles are used amongst thimble collectors as one would use business cards. The thimbles are made in the USA and are available in a variety of colours. They bear the collector's name, address and phone number and often a slogan. In Australia only a handful of collectors have had these thimbles made for themselves (in the USA), with their personal details to use when attending thimble conferences overseas. Iris Woolley is one of the few Australian collectors to use personalised thimbles.

Precision Plastics

Plastic thimbles were made by Precision Plastics Pty Ltd of Sydney. According to Woolley (1988), part of the factory that produced thimbles was destroyed by fire in 1978 and the machinery was not replaced. The factory was originally situated in Chatswood and is now operating in Castle Hill in Sydney but no thimbles are being made.

The maker's name, 'Precision Plastics Pty Ltd Sydney' and size numbering appear up inside the apex. The sizes range from 0 to 7, with size 0 being the largest. The thimbles are all of the same design and there is a choice of many bright or pastel colours in each size range. Precision Plastics' range include thimbles in lustre colours; a few mottled examples exist but these are more likely the result of poor quality control than deliberate mottling.

It is a challenge for thimble collectors today to have a complete set of Precision Plastics thimbles in all eight sizes (*Plate 37*).

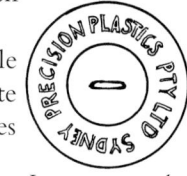

Inner apex mark

War Chest Fund

During the 1914–1918 war 13 000 white ivorine thimbles were donated by Mrs Ninian Thomson to the War Chest Thimble Fund in New South Wales to raise funds for comforts for the Australian men fighting in Europe.

The War Chest Thimble Fund was established in May 1917. By the following January 10 000 thimbles had been sold to swell the funds. The thimbles were 'sold by orders from the country and in other States, or at stands, which have been held in different parts of the city [Sydney] each week'.

Mrs Thomson bore the cost of purchasing the thimbles as well as having the lettering applied. The lettering seems to have been on paper applied to the thimbles but the records at the time (*War workers gazette 1918*) show that the lettering was done by F. W. Ward, 'engraver'.

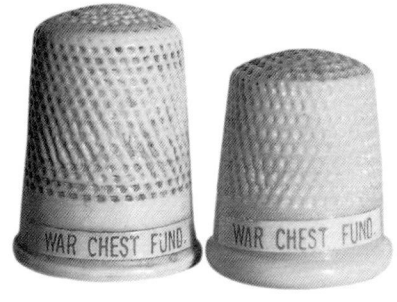

War Chest Fund ivorine thimbles 1918

The War Chest thimbles are of a creamy coloured plastic with blue lettering on white, corresponding to the colours of the War Chest Fund. Two shapes exist: a small one with a rolled rim, the other taller with a wider band. The thimbles would have been made by Charles Iles of Birmingham. Iles patented ivorine thimbles in 1913, advertising them as 'manufactured like solid ivory'. There are two styles of Iles ivorine thimbles which correspond to the two types of War Chest Fund thimbles.

These War Chest thimbles amounted to the largest volume of any one thimble to be sold in Australia, yet precious few have survived in collections.

SHELL THIMBLES

Mother-of-pearl thimbles

Broome in Western Australia is the home of Australia's pearling industry. It is appropriate that these mother-of-pearl shell thimbles, made in the 1980s, come from Broome. There are two types available, both made from pieces of shell forming a chequered pattern. The inside of the thimbles seems to be a type of light plastic. The contrasting black and cream shell combination is most striking. The thimbles have a lovely smooth feeling to them. There are no maker's marks.

Shell thimbles from Broome

Bryan Fraser

Bryan Fraser of Artistry in Brass, Caringbah, New South Wales, advertised that he made thimbles from mother-of-pearl, but no examples could be found.

STONE THIMBLES

With the abundance of semi-precious stones available in Australia, it is surprising that only a few types have found their way onto thimbles as decoration, or been used to make whole thimbles. Many thimbles have, however, been decorated with opals and are much sought after by overseas collectors. Opals were discovered in Australia in the 1870s and marketed in London from the late eighties. The principal fields are at White Cliffs and Lightning Ridge in New South Wales and Coober Pedy in South Australia. Thimbles with opals or other semi-precious stones could form a niche collection.

Gemmologists would have a field day supplying stones to be placed on the apexes of thimbles.

Chrysoprase

This green stone, sometimes known as 'Australian jade', is a variety of chalcedony found in Queensland. Thimbella had thimbles made by various woodturners to their design to take these stones and then assembled the stones on the thimbles themselves. Chrysoprase has been used on top of these Queensland maple wooden thimbles. The thimbles are un-signed. Other stones used include malachite, agate and a jade of a deep green colour found in Cowell, South Australia.

Chrysoprase on wood

Jade

The Pilbara area of Western Australia is known for its wealth of mineral resources. Jade is mined at Marble Bar at the Comet Gold Mine. The jade thimble illustrated was the first jade thimble ever produced in the Pilbara. The apex is flat and has several large indentations. There are no maker's marks (*Plate 38*).

Marble

Marble is difficult to work with as it is a very soft material that falls apart easily when being carved. Two types of South Australian marble have been made into thimbles in Whyalla in South Australia: white marble from the Barossa Valley and a harder pale green marble from Cowell. The sides of the chunky thimbles are straight and smooth and the apex is flat and cross-hatched. There are no maker's marks (*Plate 39*).

Zebra stone

Zebra stone was found in 1924 in the Kimberley Region of Western Australia, long before Lake Argyle was flooded. As the name suggests it is a striped stone, with beautiful white and red bands, formed 500 to 600 million years ago. A deposit was formed near where Kununurra is today. The sparsely distributed seams of zebra stone near Lake Argyle are the only known deposits of this remarkable material. Unfortunately only a small portion of the total deposit remains above water following the construction of Lake Argyle in 1972.

Top Rockz Gallery in Kununurra is run by John and Nancy Read. What started as a hobby on their retirement in 1987 is a successful gallery today. Having lived in the area on and off for over thirty years, John took out some leases in 1987 on special stones in inaccessible spots in the Kimberley region, including zebra stone. Their time is now divided between Kununurra and Perth. In Kununurra for the northern tourist season for the five 'dry' months between June and September of each year, the Reads have run Top Rockz Gallery since 1990, supplying handmade gifts and collectable items made from stones of the region to tourists from all over the world. John digs for stone and the stock is then created down in Perth during the balance of the year ready for the next season. The Reads also carry a range of thimbles made from beautiful woodworking timber found in the Kimberleys.

Zebra stone is soft enough to cut and carve with handtools; it has a smooth silky texture but is fragile. The thimbles are beautifully marked with red-brown streaks on a beige background. The thimbles are available with or without copper studs that are situated up in the apex. These studs protect the tops of the stone thimbles, which would otherwise split whilst sewing. The thimbles are unmarked, but their very uniqueness surely makes this unnecessary.

Zebra stone

SEWING KITS

Sewing kits, consisting of a thimble and needle container/cotton winder, have been made since the 1920s. They were often made as giveaways. The earlier kits would have been made of metal, the later ones of plastic.

Bushells Blue Label Tea

As well as thimbles, Bushells commissioned advertising sewing kits. These aluminium tubular kits have an aluminium thimble as the lid. The thimbles have 'Bushells Blue Label Tea' lettered around a blue band, with 'German Make' stamped into the indentations and a blue glass top. An 'Austrian Make' thimble will not fit these German made sewing kits. The thimble lifts off to reveal a wooden needlecase/thread winder inside. The base of the sewing tube has a motif of a horseshoe enclosing a four-leafed clover.

Bushells Blue Label Tea sewing kit

Gramp's Orlando Wines

Sewing kits advertising South Australia's Gramp's Orlando Wines are made in the shape of a wine bottle. The thimble forms the base of the kit; there is a thread holder with a needlecase inside, and a pencil fits in the neck of the bottle. The kits were made in Germany.

Greater Newcastle Permanent

These modern sewing kits are used as advertising giveaways. The plastic kits are rectangular and all of the same colour. The thimbles are also rectangular

Modern sewing kit

OTHER THIMBLES

in shape and fit in the end of the kits. The kits contain a cotton winder with a needleholder housed in the centre. The lettering is gilt on black with 'Compliments of Greater Newcastle Permanent'. There are probably other sewing kits available in Australia with advertisements.

Kurant

From the 1920s to the 1950s Kurant made plastic sewing kits. They were not made in Australia but have been found with several Australian place names. The cream plastic tubular kits have variously coloured plastic screw-on thimbles. They all bear a metal or plastic disc on the tube, showing various tourist destinations. There is a ring with a silk tassel on the end of each kit. Above this ring is the maker's mark in raised lettering, but being the same colour as the body is difficult to detect. The kits also contain a cotton winder with a needleholder in the centre.

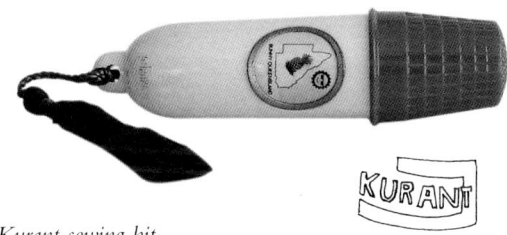

Kurant sewing kit

"La Perle" Perfumes

Metal kits in the form of a tube exist advertising "La Perle" Perfumes. A brass thimble forms the top of the sewing kit and the contents are a cotton winder/ needleholder. The red metal tubular body is lettered 'With the Compliments of the Perfumes "La Perle" Perfume Prestre & Co Sydney'. There are no maker's marks on the kits to identify where they were made.

"La Perle" Perfumes Sydney sewing kit

MISCELLANEOUS

Fridge magnets

In 1989 the Needlework Tool Collectors Society of Australia had a consignment of 250 fridge magnets made to raise funds for their first Corroboree, held in Melbourne in 1990. They proved so popular that a similar order was placed by the Society the following year. These 40 mm x 44 mm ($1^5/_8$" x 1¾") flat 'Aussie Fridge Magnets', produced by Perfection Plate Holdings of Revesby in Sydney, illustrate the Nifty thimble on a red background. In the October 1989 issue of *TCI Bulletin* these refrigerator magnets were offered for sale, thus swelling the fundraising effort beyond Australia's borders.

Nifty fridge magnet

Postcards

The Needlework Tool Collectors Society of Australia had a stunning set of six postcards made for sale to the delegates at their first Corroboree in 1990. On a deep red background the postcards illustrate six sewing tools, including one design showing a silver Nifty thimble. The photographs were taken by Katrina Cowen, who was the secretary of the Society at the time. One thousand sets were ordered. It is significant that the Society chose to incorporate the Nifty thimble on two promotional items.

Nifty postcard for Needlework Tool Collectors Society of Australia

Thimble boxes and thimble holders

Thimble boxes and containers have been around since thimbles became more than just an item of sewing necessity. In the nineteenth century thimble boxes came into their own and are found in as many different mediums as there are thimbles. Thimble containers are collectables in their own right.

PORCELAIN THIMBLE HOLDERS

Lynn Richards Porcelain
Lynn Richards, of the Gold Coast in Queensland, makes porcelain thimble holders to house her handpainted porcelain thimbles. Since meeting with Sue Gowan in 1993, Lynn has evolved moulds for a variety of thimble holders. The holders are handpainted to match the thimbles, identical in every detail. No two holders or thimbles are the same.

Richards' range presently contains egg-shaped, shoe and pink ballet shoe thimble holders. As with all her pink or cream porcelain work and handpainting, Lynn's thimble holders with their pastel floral designs and 24 carat gold trims are collectors' items. Each bears the lettering 'Lynn Richards Australia' on the holder plus her personal numbering system identifying the colour of the holder, the specific shape and the particular design. This numbering system enables collectors to build up a matching set of any chosen design over time.

Lynn has also produced sewing sets with a handpainted matching thimble and tape-measure container on a small tray, with a matching pincushion in a shoe. The round, lidded tape-measure boxes have a slit in the porcelain to allow the tape-measure to be pulled through.

Porcelain sewing set by Lynn Richards of the Gold Coast

Egg thimble-container with matching thimble handpainted by Lynn Richards

AUSTRALIAN JEWELLERS' THIMBLE BOXES
In the absence of an established Australian thimble industry, local jewellers had thimble boxes made with their names inside. Most of the boxes that have survived date from the 1910s and 1920s, as the thimbles seem mainly to be the original occupants. It is not important which thimbles were sold with the box, suffice to say they were all imported, with no connection with Australia. Some are sturdy, others are of cardboard, but the fact that they have survived, some in pristine condition, is a credit to their early owners.

These are some of the Australian jewellers who had thimble boxes made to sell thimbles; the list reads like a Who's Who of early twentieth century

Australian jewellers. The inverted commas enclose the exact wording in or on each box or case.

'**Caris Bros.** London & Coolgardie W.A.' is lettered in gold inside the lid. The case is of black faux leather, velvet lined, fastening with a metal clip. Caris Bros were jewellers in Perth and Kalgoorlie as well; the Coolgardie branch would have had a very brief existence. Stanley Caris started as an importer of jewellery in Coolgardie in 1894 (Erickson 1989) and coincidentally the thimble in the thimble box cited dates from 1894.

Caris Bros. Coolgardie

'**Amos Corbett** Leichhardt St Waverley'. There is no mention of Amos Corbett in Cavill (1992), so one presumes that this Melbourne jeweller used no recognisable marks on his jewellery. This thimble case has a domed lid, fastening with a metal clip and the silk and velvet lined case is lettered on the inside of the lid.

Amos Corbett Waverley

'**Stewart Dawson & Co.** Diamond Merchants Manufacturing Jewellers Sidney [sic] Melbourne, Auckland and Perth'. Their flagship store was in Melbourne, initially in Swanston Street and then at 234 Collins Street until 1947.

Stewart Dawson

'**W Dunkling** 317 Bourke Street Melbourne Watchmaker Jeweller' is lettered in gold inside the lid. The case is of brown leather with blue velvet lining and has a metal fastening. Dunklings are still trading in Melbourne (*Plate 40*).

'**Flavelle Brothers Ltd.** Sydney & London English Made Case Estd 1846' is lettered inside the case: a

Flavelle Brothers Sydney

maroon leather case with a satin and velvet lining. Flavelle Brothers operated as a limited company in Sydney between 1888 and 1921.

'**Flavelle Bros & Roberts** Sydney Brisbane' is inside the lid of this unusual bell-shaped thimble container made of turquoise leather and silk. According to Cavill (1992), the jewellers bearing this name were in business in Sydney from 1869–1887 and 1870–1891 in Brisbane, making this the oldest known thimble case with an Australian jeweller's inscription to have survived.

'**Hardy Bros. Ltd.** 13 Hunter St. Sydney and 118 Queen St. Brisbane Made in England' is lettered inside the lid. The black case is satin and green velvet lined, similar to the Flavelle Bros box. Hardy Bros were at both these addresses from 1894.

Another example is a thimble box with 'Hardy Bros. Ltd Jewellers & Silversmiths Australia Made in England' lettered inside the lid. The box is larger, with gilt edging, and older, without the specific addresses.

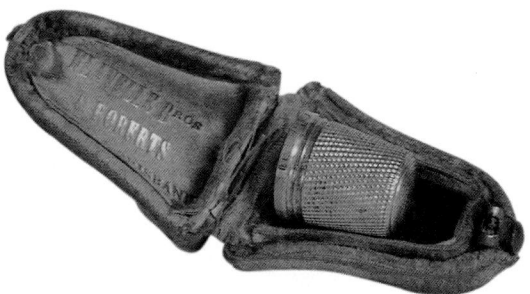

Flavelle Bros & Roberts Sydney & Brisbane

Hardy Bros Sydney & Brisbane

'**Flavelle, Roberts & Sankey Ltd.** Sydney, Brisbane, Rockhampton & Lismore.' is lettered inside the little cardboard Royal Worcester box. This is the only thimble box known to have survived with an Australiana thimble: the 1926 Royal Worcester kookaburra thimble (page 56) belongs in this box. This firm of jewellers opened their Lismore branch in 1922, long after their Rockhampton (1896), Sydney (1856) and Brisbane (1892) branches, so thimble boxes with inscriptions for all four branches are rare (*Plate 41*).

'**Gunter's** 237 Bourke St Melbourne'. The lettering is very worn on this green thimble box, being on the outside. Gunter's only existed at this address between 1906 and 1915 (*Plate 42*).

'**Anthony Hordern & Sons** Palace Emporium Sydney'. Hordens were in the Haymarket in Sydney between 1869 and 1950. The box is a beige cardboard one, with the lettering on the outside lid. The thimble dates to 1913 (*Plate 43*).

'**C. Jensen** Watchmaker & Jeweller Tenterfield'. Jensen worked as jeweller in Tenterfield, New South Wales, between 1901 and 1929. It is wonderful to discover a thimble box from a relatively small country community. The cardboard box is beige in colour with the lettering on the outside lid, similar to the Hordern box.

Jensen Tenterfield

'**Prouds Ltd** cor. Pitt & King Sts Sydney. Watchmakers & Jewellers' is lettered inside the lid. The blue case is lined with satin and velvet. The thimble can be dated to 1925, which according to Cavill (1992) falls within the period when Prouds were substantially established at that address. Prouds stores are still in operation throughout Australia.

Prouds Sydney

'**Stevenson Bros** 20, Rundle St., Adelaide. Watchmakers & Jewellers. Made in England'. Walter and William Stevenson were jewellers in Adelaide from 1878 and operated at 20 Rundle Street from the 1890s until 1956. The thimble box is of cardboard and is lettered on the inside lid.

Stevenson Bros Adelaide

'**J C Taylor Pty Ltd** 704 Hay Street Perth WA' was a jeweller in Perth between 1905 and 1935. The box is of cardboard with a pink and grey pattern with the lettering in blue on the outside lid.

J M Wendt Several different thimble boxes from this well-known Adelaide jeweller have survived. All are lettered on the outside and this has tended to wear off the lettering. One example is a brown cardboard box with lettering 'J M Wendt Adelaide Foreign made box'; another is 'J M Wendt Jeweller Adelaide' on a blue cardboard box; and 'J. M. Wendt Adelaide. German Made Box' in gold lettering appears on a blue cardboard thimble box with a 1899 thimble. Wendts have been jewellers in Adelaide since 1854. Joachim Matthias Wendt, the founder of the current firm, died in 1917, so these boxes would be from prior to that date.

Wendt Adelaide

'"My Jeweller" **Harry Young** 526 George St Sydney' is lettered inside this very small thimble box. Youngs operated at this address from 1903 until the 1950s.

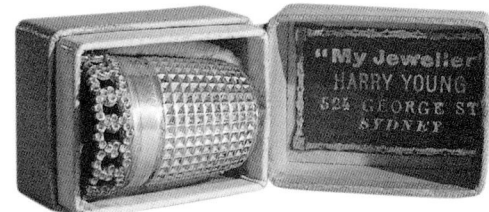

Harry Young Sydney

Appendix

APPENDIX 1 Australian thimble marks

1 Aronson & Co.	S·S ACo	*9 James Cumberland-Brown*	J.F.C.
2 "AUSSIE"	S·S ⬠ S·L "AUSSIE		
3 Australian Impressions (Fauna/Western Australia)	AUSTRALIAN IMPRESSIONS FINE BONE CHINA	*10 Elfin*	2 ELFIN STG.SIL
4 Australian Impressions (Flora)	AUSTRALIAN TASMANIAN BLUE GUM TASMANIA IMPRESSIONS FINE BONE CHINA	*11 Pat Hagan*	STERLING Nº 20
		12 Ian Hannay	VA
5 August Brunkhorst	BRUNKHORST ADELAIDE		
6 Cabochon	HAHNDORF THE Cabochon COLLECTION AUSTRALIA	*13 Curtis Hine*	H.C.H STG.SIL
		14 Pat Holcombe	STERLING
7 Eric Car	⑨ SSr 🦘	*15 Impress Ceramics*	IMPRESS CERAMICS COWES PHILLIP ISLAND VIC. 3922 AUSTRALIA
8 Frank Cowan	STG SIL  L		

APPENDIX

16 Daniel Jenkins	 925
17 Rod Kranz	℞ 925
18 Kyneton Fine China	*Kyneton Fine China* MADE IN AUSTRALIA
19 Zygmunt L	ZL 925
20 Liberty Lane	*Liberty Lane Australia*
21 Tony Lievesly	TL 78
22 R.P.A. Matho-Dudare	 St. Sil *matho* 8/97 STG SIL Mϕ 9/ϕ
23 Nifty sterling silver	•NIFTY• STG. SILVER 8
24 Nifty 9ct silver-lined	9CT SIL LINED (NIFTY) 7
25 Ray Norman	STG. SIL
26 Syd Oates	STG.SIL 9
27 Palfrey 9ct gold (1)	PALFREY 
28 Palfrey 9ct gold (2)	 PALFREY
29 Pan Arts (Birchcroft)	
30 Pan Arts (Ken Parry)	PAN ARTS COLLECTABLES SYDNEY - AUSTRALIA ENGLISH BONE CHINA
31 Pan Arts pewter (old)	PAN ARTS SYDNEY ©
32 Pan Arts pewter (new)	
33 N. Parker	925 N.C.P. 88.
34 Platypus Gallery	PLATYPUS GALLERY MADE IN WALES

35 Precision Plastics

36 Price & Jardine
9ct gold
P.J.P   10   9   ·375   E

37 William Robinson
WR AUSTRALIAN MADE

38 John Storm
9CT   *JS*

39 John Tarasin
JRT   9ct S|S

40 Marylyn Verstraeten

41 Christian Vocke
 AUSTRALIA

42 Malcolm Walter
  925

43 Westminster China (Flora/Fauna)

Westminster
TASMANIA
STATE FLOWER
AUSTRALIA

44 Westminster China (Tribal Man)

© 1995 TOBWABBA ART
Authentic Australian Aboriginal Art
Tribal Man - G 2571

APPENDIX 2 Koalas on thimbles

Koalas are portrayed on more thimbles than any other design in Australia. Along with kangaroos, they are difficult to represent accurately. Judge for yourself the differing standards on the following thimbles, where some koalas are realistically depicted and others look more like monkeys.

K1 *Australian Impressions and Platypus Gallery*

K2 *Birchcroft*

K3 *Regal and Caverswall*

K4 *Franklin Mint and Westminster*

K5 *Pan Arts 'No worries'*

K6 Pan Arts 'Australian Tea Ceremony'

K7 Pan Arts

K8 Pan Arts' Sun-Herald Koala Fund

K9 Handpainted by Pat Adam

K10 Handpainted

K12 Swagman Pottery

K13 Firehydrant

K11 Caroline Cameron's breaddough

Appendix

K14 Firehydrant

K15 Koala Cottage Ginger Factory

K16 Taiwan blank

K17 Taiwan blank

K18 Taiwan blank

K19 Taiwan blank

K20 Taiwan blank

K21 Taiwan blank

112 *Thimbles of Australia*

K22 *Taiwan blank*

K23 *Taiwan blank*

K24 *Buckingham Pewter*

K25 *Exquisite Pewter*

K26 *Pewter from Japan*

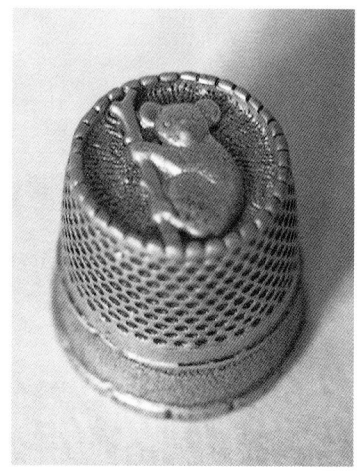
K27 *Fort Pewter*

K28 *Pan Arts pewter and Stephen Frost*

K29 *Pan Arts pewter*

APPENDIX 113

K30 *Miniature Kingdom*

K31 *Pan Arts pewter*

K32 *Riccardo's pewter*

K33 *Marylyn Verstraeten*

K34 *Robert Herron*

K35 *Handpainted by Margaret Greschke*

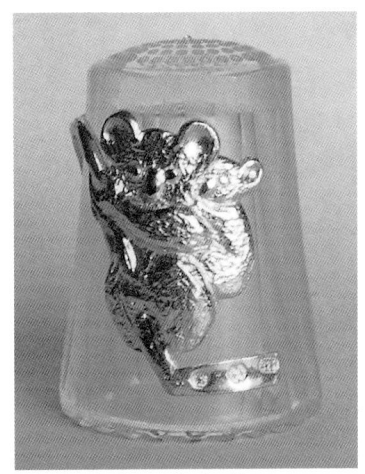

K37 *Malcolm Walter's silver over crystal*

K36 *Peter Grossman's pewter, handpainted base by Ann Wallace*

K38 *Papier-mâché by Haley and cattle horn by John Trier*

K39 *Scrimshaw by James Cumberland-Brown*

K40 *Papier-mâché by Haley*

APPENDIX 3 China painters and woodturners

Dates and places are included where known, usually from their inclusion on the thimbles.

China painters

Andrews, J.B.—Sydney
Arnold, A.—Western Australia
Bayliss, Jocelyn—Queensland
Bedingfield, Jo—Sydney 1987
Brook, Marj
Brown, Heather
Brown, Pat—Adelaide
Brunton, Helen
Buck, Pam—Hahndorf SA
Campbell, Gwen—Queensland
Campbell, Joan
Campbell, Megan R.—Sydney 1981
Carriage, N.—Canberra
Cartledge, Ruth
Christie, Peg—Brisbane
Covill, Mary—1988
Cynthia—Toowoomba
Dante
Davies, Helen
Drok, Kitty
Dyer, Judy—Melbourne 1976
Faris, N.
Faulks, Margaret
Fleming-Tatura, V.
Fraser, J.
Freeman, N.
Gabb, Gay
Gallagher, Mabs—Canberra 1990
Gamble, J.—Sydney
Gavin, W.
Gooden, Alma
Gould, Georgina
Gregory, J.
Griffiths, Fay
Gumley, Olive
Haley, William (Bill)—New Zealand 1988
Hammich, Althea—Nambucca Heads NSW
Haysman, B.
Holland, Roma
Hulbert, Marilyn
Hunter, P.—Tanunda SA 1996
Jones, Margaret
Laverty, Maureen—Brisbane 1995
Lyndon, Pat—Manly NSW
Marlborough, Deidre—Newcastle NSW
Matthews, I.
McCormack, Carol
Moree—Coburn
Moyle, J.
Nock, Joan—Perth 1994
Noel, Joy—Brisbane 1996
Pardon, H—Sydney 1988
Patterson, Roma
Pope, J
Prentice, Roma
Pritchard, Julie
Rains, S.
Reid, Gillem—New Norfolk Tasmania
Riley, Geoff—Melbourne 1940–1960s
Sanders, Lee—Kadina SA
Saunders, E.—Sydney
Schubert, Jan
Searle, M.—Western Australia
Sherwood, L.A.—Perth
Simpson, C.
Stanger, Thelma—1986
Tesdariero, Elva
Tuck, P.
Turner, Merle—Adelaide 1988
Vargo, Jill
Wyatt, F.—Western Australia

Woodturners

The following turners are known to have made wooden thimbles.

Anderson, Syd—Qld
Barnes, Eric—WA
Bickett, Vic—Vic
Boyd, Elaine—WA
Bretag
Brittain, Ray—Qld
Brooks, John—WA
Carmichael, Alan
Clarke, Jim—WA
Collings—SA
Cranville, Greg—SA
Cumberland-Brown, James—WA
Dunn, Dave—SA
Ellison, Harry—SA
Garth, Ian—Vic
Hallows, Mal—Qld
Harper, Lewis—Vic
Hardie, Roy—Qld
Kettle, Tom—WA
Keynes, Don—WA
McLaren, Dave—SA
McQueen, Keith—WA
Meldrum, Alex—WA
Neve, Toni—Vic
Nicholls, Len—WA
Osmond, J.
Smith, Ron—WA
Sauter, Franz—Vic
St Clair, Mike—Canberra ACT
Syme, Lynn—Qld
Webb, Mark
Wyer, Peter—Qld

APPENDIX 4 Pan Arts China Thimbles

Australia Series
No 1   Kangaroo (Ken Parry) (sold out)
No 2   Kookaburra
No 3   Koala
No 4   Native flowers
No 5   Sydney Harbour Bridge New South Wales
No 6   Sydney Opera House (Ken Parry) (sold out)
No 7   Great Barrier Reef, Queensland
No 8   Ayers Rock, Northern Territory
No 9   Sulphur-crested cockatoo
No 10   Platypus
No 11   Black swans
No 12   Wombat
No 13   Advance Australia Fair 1788-1988 (sold out)
No 14   The Three Sisters
No 15   Bound for Australia (with blue flags)
        Bound for Australia (with yellow flags)
No 16   Sydney Cove 1788
No 17   Lyrebird
No 18   Fairy penguin
No 19   Kangaroos
No 20   Sydney Opera House
No 21   Echidna
no 22   Advance Australia Fair (with flags, no date)
no 23   Melbourne Victoria
No 24   Parliament House Canberra
No 25   No Worries (Kate Burness)
No 26   Australian Tea Ceremony (Kate Burness)
No 27   Rosellas
No 28   Sydney Sesquicentenary
No 29   Sydney Town Hall
No 30   Swan family
No 31   Superb blue wren
No 32   King parrot (same as Signature Series No 2)
No 33   Green & golden bull frog
No 34   *Endeavour* & Cook
No 35   Olympic Opera House
No 36   Olympic frogs
No 37   Koala Australia
No 38   Sydney Welcomes the Year 2000
No 39   Australia Welcomes the Year 2001

Australian Endangered Species/ WWF (World Wildlife Fund)
Frogs (4)
Eucalypts (4)
Butterflies (3)
Possums (2)
Numbat
Ghost bat
Ground parrot
Paradise parrot
Helmeted honeyeater
Forty-spotted pardalote
Thylacine (Tasmanian tiger)
Freshwater crocodile
Snakes and lizards (8)
Western swamp tortoise
Northern hairy-nosed wombat
Sooty owl and plumed frogmouth
Rare or threatened orchids (16)
Threatened wattles–Acacias (7)
Golden-shouldered and hooded parrots
Greater bilby and Western barred bandicoot
Banded hare-wallaby and bridled nail-tailed wallaby
Proteaceae—Banksias and Grevilleas
Corals and Creatures—The Great Barrier Reef
'SOS'—Awareness Appreciation Protection Preservation
Gungurra—*Eucalyptus caesia*

Endangered and Threatened Species/WWF (World Wildlife Fund) in Resin
Gouldian finch
Purple-crowned fairy wren
Princess parrot
Sooty owl
Lithochroa Blue
Amaryllis Azure
Fiery Jewel
Pale Cerulean
Regent Skipper
Honey possum
Mountain pygmy possum
The Great Barrier Reef

Signature Bird Series (Australian Native Birds Collection) 1990
No 1   Eclectus parrot
No 2   King parrot (same as Australia Series No 32)
No 3   Rosella parrots
No 4   Gang-gang cockatoo
No 5   Sulphur-crested cockatoo
No 6   Wedge-tailed eagle
No 7   Australian owls
No 8   Brolga
No 9   Black swan
No 10   Kingfishers
No 11   Honey-eaters
No 12   Superb blue wren

Special Series (only available from the advertised place)
S1   Sydney Opera House
S2   Ginninderra Village Canberra, A.C.T.
S3   Blackheath Blue Mountains N.S.W. (rhododendrons)
S4   *The Sun-Herald* Koala Fund (1989)
S5   Queen Victoria Building (for Koala Bear Shop in the QVB)
S6   Hall Village ACT
S7   Parliament House Canberra
S8   Werribee Park (Victoria)
S9   Kangaroo Valley New South Wales Australia (1990)
S10 Greetings from Bowral N.S.W. (tulips)
S11 National Gallery of Australia (painting—never released)
S12 Melbourne Quilt Exhibition (1992—issued without the number)

- S13 Blue Mountains Australia (crimson rosellas)
- S14 Mooloolaba Queensland Australia (Mooloolah on the Spit)
- S15 Scenic Skyway Katoomba
- S16 O'Reillys Lamington National Park Queensland
- S17 Healesville Sanctuary (their logo available with other Pan Arts fauna designs—not issued with the number)
- S18 Uluru Australia's Northern Territory (issued without the number)
- S19 Kings Canyon Watarrka National Park Australia (issued without the number)
- S20 Queensland Quilters Inc 1997 (issued without the number)

APPENDIX 5 Advertisements and Gibson's patent

Nifty

Price & Jardine manufactured articles in 9 carat gold, 9 carat silver lined, silver, chromium plate and stainless steel. They made in many designs in the following range, in rough chronological order: bangles, rings, hairpins, studs, armlets, bracelets, golf bangles, 'Gumnut' lucky charms, brooches, Nifty silver comforters, silver and gold golf pencils, lockets, cufflinks, novelty bookmarkers, golf links, teething rings, silver rattles, spoons and pushers, armlets, Mother brooches, collar pins, chain bangles, key brooches for 21st birthdays, souvenir brooches for 150th anniversary (of the founding of Australia), nail files, necklets, pendants, crosses, Army, Navy and Airforce badges in 1941, fobs, sleeve links, tie holders, badges, teaspoons with Australian animals, kookaburra brooches and 'Kidikin' children's jewellery, but their main line was flexible watch bands.

All the above bore the 'Nifty' trademark, were made in Australia and supplied through the wholesale and retail trade.

Nifty and Elfin advertisements

Nifty silver thimble advertised

Appendix

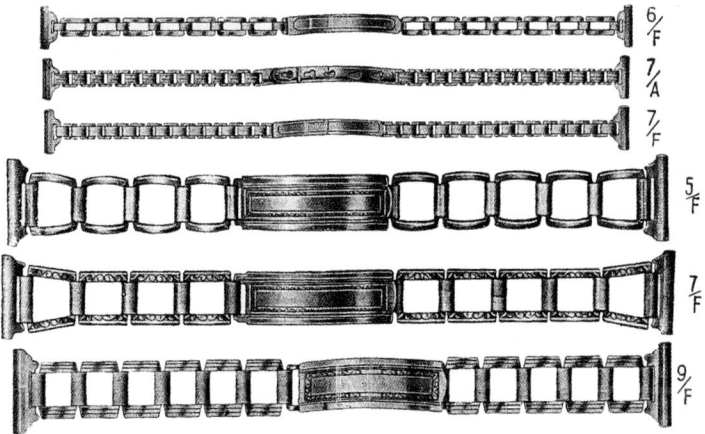

A second Nifty silver thimble advertisement

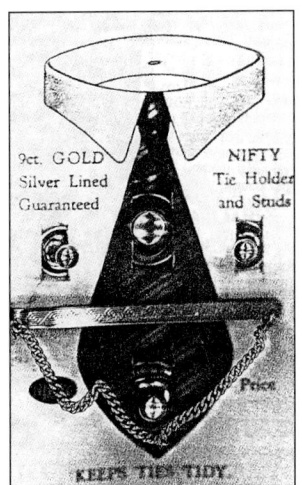

Tie set: An actual Nifty tie holder and studs

First Roy Humphery advertisement (Commonwealth Jeweller and Watchmaker June 1946)

"NIFTY" CURB CHAIN BANGLES

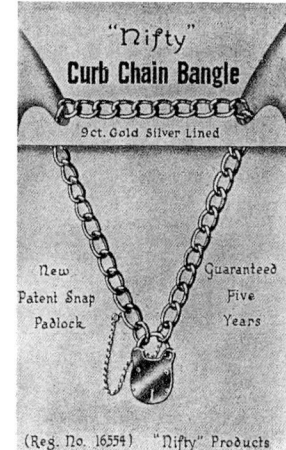

COVERED WITH
1/10th 9 CARAT GOLD
SILVER LINING.

Guaranteed
5 YEARS

A QUALITY PRODUCT
WHICH WILL GIVE
SATISFACTORY
SERVICE.

REGISTERED
PATENT PADLOCK
CLOSES
WITH SPRING.

PERFECTLY SECURE.

WILL STAY CLOSED
UNTIL OPENED BY
PRESSING
CATCH ON SIDE.

"NIFTY" LADIES AND GENT.'S FLEXIBLE WATCH BANDS
Made in 9 ct. Gold, 9 ct. Silver-Lined and Nickel.
Equal in Quality to the World's Best. Large Assortment of Designs.

OTHER QUALITY PRODUCTS MANUFACTURED BY "NIFTY"—

9ct. Silver-Lined GOLD BANGLES and ARMLETS
9ct. Gold and Silver-Lined BROOCHES, COLLAR PINS
TIE HOLDERS with CHAIN, SLEEVE LINKS, ONE PIECE STUDS.
Real Silver Golf Pencils, Comforters, Nail Files, Rattles, Thimbles, Spoons and Pushers, etc., etc.

"NIFTY" PRODUCTS ✦ 431 Elizabeth St., SYDNEY

THE COMMONWEALTH JEWELLER and WATCHMAKER — July 9, 1938.

The last mention of Nifty silver thimbles

ROY A. HUMPHERY
Wholesale Jeweller and Importer
92 PITT STREET, SYDNEY

Ring Clips for quick sizing of rings — in White or Yellow Gold.

IMMEDIATE
DELIVERY
FOR
BOTH LINES

Sterling Silver Thimbles with Steel Reinforced Ends — attractively boxed in one dozen lots. Assorted sizes.

'Phone: BW8429 ——————— Your Orders

November 10, 1947.   THE COMMONWEALTH JEWELLER AND WATCHMAKER.   Page Ninety-seven

This advertisement ran monthly till July 1948

Appendix

A general advertisement from Roy Humphery in which the illustration of the Elfin thimble appeared regularly until April 1950

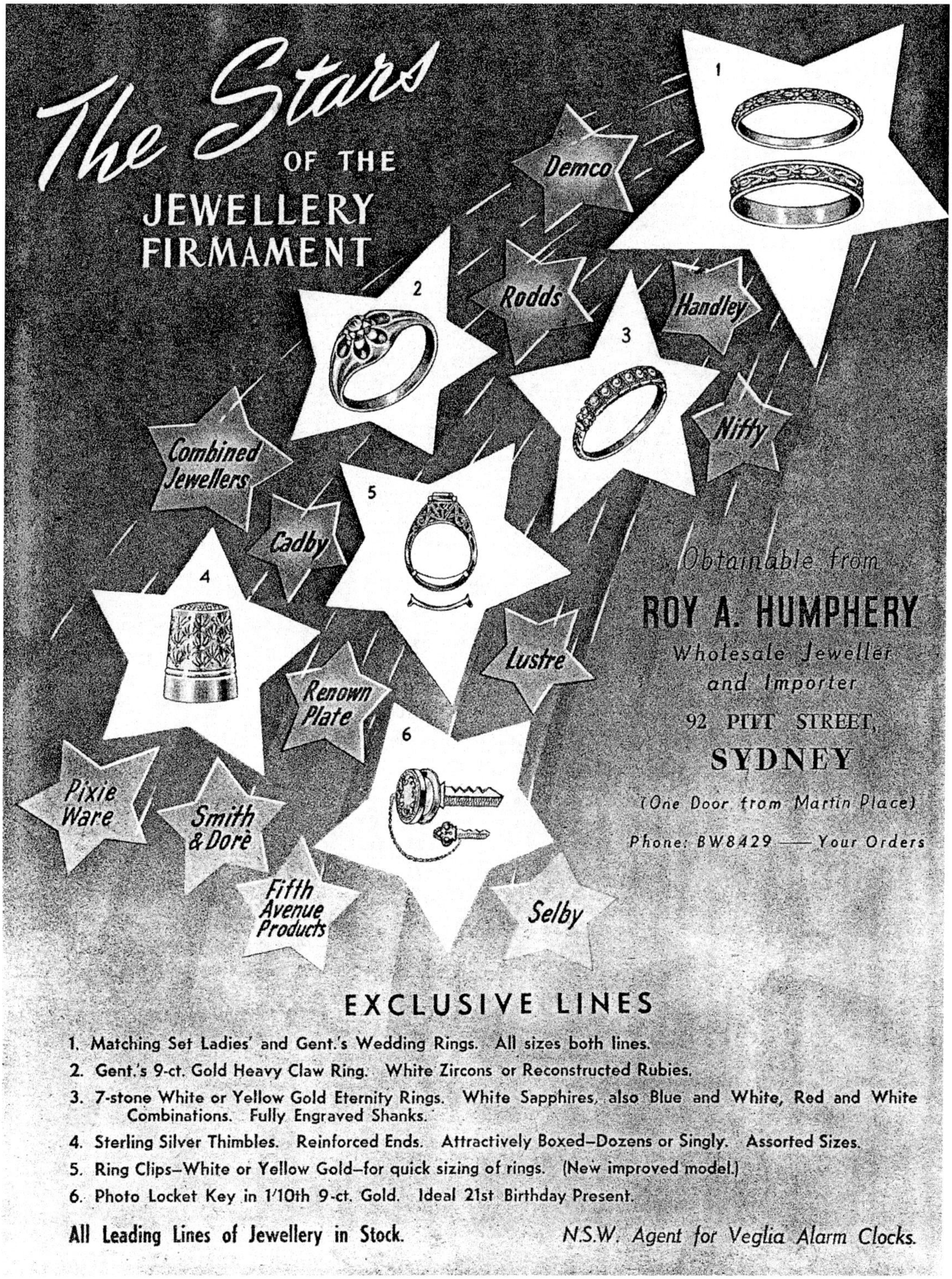

The Stars OF THE JEWELLERY FIRMAMENT

1. Demco
2. Rodds
3. Handley — Nifty
4. Combined Jewellers — Cadby
5. (ring)
6. Pixie Ware — Renown Plate — Smith & Doré — Lustre — Fifth Avenue Products — Selby

Obtainable from

ROY A. HUMPHERY
Wholesale Jeweller and Importer
92 PITT STREET, SYDNEY
(One Door from Martin Place)
Phone: BW8429 —— Your Orders

EXCLUSIVE LINES

1. Matching Set Ladies' and Gent.'s Wedding Rings. All sizes both lines.
2. Gent.'s 9-ct. Gold Heavy Claw Ring. White Zircons or Reconstructed Rubies.
3. 7-stone White or Yellow Gold Eternity Rings. White Sapphires, also Blue and White, Red and White Combinations. Fully Engraved Shanks.
4. Sterling Silver Thimbles. Reinforced Ends. Attractively Boxed—Dozens or Singly. Assorted Sizes.
5. Ring Clips—White or Yellow Gold—for quick sizing of rings. (New improved model.)
6. Photo Locket Key in 1/10th 9-ct. Gold. Ideal 21st Birthday Present.

All Leading Lines of Jewellery in Stock.   N.S.W. Agent for Veglia Alarm Clocks.

Page 94 — THE COMMONWEALTH JEWELLER AND WATCHMAKER — August 10, 1948.

Alexander Gibson's patent

No. 18,302/15.

APPLICATION DATED

31st December, 1915.

Applicant (Actual Inventor)	ALEXANDER GIBSON.
Application and Provisional Specification ...	Lodged 31st December, 1915.
Application and Provisional Specification ...	Accepted 22nd September, 1916.
Complete Specification	Lodged 31st August, 1916.
Complete Specification Accepted 23rd Oct., 1916	Acceptance Advertised (Sec. 50) 8 Nov., 1916.

Class 42.1.

Drawing attached.

COMPLETE SPECIFICATION.

"Improvements in and relating to thimbles."

I, ALEXANDER GIBSON, of Rosebrook, Port Fairy, in the State of Victoria, Commonwealth of Australia, Traveller, hereby declare this invention and the manner in which
5 it is to be performed, to be fully described and ascertained in and by the following statement:—

This invention relates to improvements in thimbles used by seamstresses, tailors and
10 others in sewing and which are intended to protect the finger when pressure is placed on the needle.

At present, in sewing processes the cotton thread has to be broken or cut when the work
15 in hand is complete, and this necessitates the use of scissors or other means involving putting down the needle and making a break in the work.

It is to overcome this that my invention
20 has been devised, according to which I provide a thimble, which may have the ordinary pitted spherical surface or a number of pitted flat facets, with a slot containing a small knife blade that is adapted to slide
25 therein and project through a narrow slit in the head of the thimble.

But in order to fully understand the invention reference is made to the accompanying drawings in which:—
30 Figure 1 is an elevation of an ordinary thimble fitted with my improvement.

Figure 2 is a sectional plan on line A-B of Figure 1, and

Figure 3 is a like view to Figure 1 but showing a thimble having a number of flat facets. 5

The thimble **4** is made with an inner lining **5** the outer part being pitted as shown and provided with the longitudinal slot **6** running nearly the whole length of the outer casing or thimble proper. At the upper end the 10 slot is closed but beyond it, in the thimble a slit **7** is made, in the same line as the slot. The latter contains the knife blade **8** which should be made of the best steel and slides in the slot longitudinally. The blade has 15 attached to it a knob or grip coming through the slot and by means of which it can be moved as required. One way of providing such a part is to nick the rear end of the blade and turn up a piece as **9** to come 20 through the slot. The blade should further be slightly bent inwards in order that, when it is sheathed in the thimble, it will bite the slit and so be held therein.

The blade is about the same length as the 25 slot and when the part **9** is at the lower end of same the knife will be within the thimble, but when the piece **9** is pushed upwards the blade will pass through the slit **7** and project from the thimble as shown. 30

18,302/15.   Thimbles.   31 Dec., 1915.

In that position it will be used by the person sewing to cut the thread when the work in hand is complete, or for other purposes such as for removing the threads that temporarily held the pieces together, without removing the thimble from the finger.

The slot and contained blade is applied to the ordinary thimble as shown in Figure 1 or to a thimble as illustrated in Figure 3 wherein are a number of facets 10 each of which is a plane superficies. By means of same a more certain hold is provided for the needle head and when pressure is applied to force the needle through the work it will be less likely to slip. Around the top of the thimble there may be a small rolled edge that projects slightly and so further contributes to prevent the needle, when pressed, from slipping off the side of the thimble.

When the blade 8 is within the slot and not projecting, the thimble will be similar to the ordinary article and will be used as such. When, however, the blade can be useful to the seamstress the blade is pushed outwards without removing the thimble from the finger and used to sever the thread or for other purposes as indicated while it remains on the finger.

Having now fully described and ascertained my said invention and the manner in which it is to be performed, I declare that what I claim is:—

1. In a thimble of the kind indicated, an inner lining, an outer casing fitted closely over the lining and slotted longitudinally, a knife blade in and contained within the slot, means for moving the blade up and down the slot and a slit in the head of the thimble beyond the end of and in line with the slot, as set forth.

2. In a thimble of the kind indicated, an inner lining, an outer casing fitted over the lining, said casing being formed either with a curved surface or with a number of facets each a plane superficies, there being in the casing a longitudinal slot and a knife blade contained within and adapted to be moved in the slot to project through an opening in the head of the thimble casing, as specified.

3. A thimble of the kind indicated and as claimed in Claims 1 and 2 having a blade bent slightly inwards so that when the blade is drawn into the thimble it will, by virtue of its slight curve, bear upon the edge of the slit in the thimble and be held therein, as set forth.

Dated this 30th day of August, 1916.

ALEXANDER GIBSON,
By his Patent Attorney,
P. M. NEWTON.

Witness—D. Crowther.

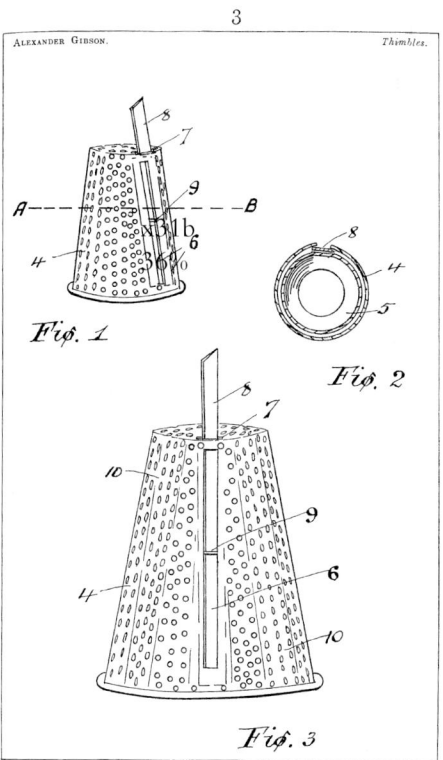

MELBOURNE WAREHOUSE

SYDNEY WAREHOUSE

MELBOURNE :
297-9 Little Collins Street.

SYDNEY :
56 York Street.

LONDON: 26 Fore Street.

ARONSON AND CO. PROPRIETARY LIMITED, finding the demand for their manufactures to be steadily increasing in South Australia, and that it has become necessary to inaugurate a quicker and more convenient method of supplying them, have opened a branch in Adelaide for the convenience of South Australian buyers. The support hitherto afforded us in this State has been very gratifying, and our efforts in the future will be directed to a still closer study of the requirements of this State.

Aronson and Company
Wholesale

BRISBANE:
173 Elizabeth Street.

ADELAIDE:
Cr. Hindley and Gresham Streets.

Our reputation in the Australian jewellery trade has been firmly established for over half-a-century, and this has been made manifest by the necessity for opening separate establishments in the capitals of the different States.

The Adelaide branch will be under the management of Mr. H. G. D. Burston, who is well and most favourably known, and customers may feel quite certain that all business will receive prompt and careful attention.

Proprietary Limited.
Jewellers.

APPENDIX 6 Chronology of jewellers, silversmiths and china manufacturers

1629	*Batavia* wrecked
1788	Settlement of Australia
1839–1930	James Fenton thimble manufacturers
1850–1962	Gabler Bros thimble manufacturers
1858–1956	Henry Griffith [& Son] thimble manufacturers
1865–1931	Henry Williamson Ltd wholesalers
1875–1919	August L. Brunkhorst
1879—	J. & W. Stewart
1880s	Hallmarking in Britain on silver thimbles
1883—	Fairfax & Roberts
1884–1947	Dorcas thimbles
1887—	James Swann [& Son] thimble manufacturers
1896–1924	George Palfrey
1899–1903	Fairfax & Roberts silver thimbles
1900 May	Empire thimble registered
1901 January	Queen Victoria died
	Federation of Australia
1901–1929	C. Jensen Tenterfield jeweller
1902–1930	Aronson & Co.
1903	Hallmarks registered in Victoria
1903–1904	Delarue silver thimbles
1904–1925	Delarue Ltd
1908	James Fenton's Queensland thimbles
1913	Charles Iles ivorine thimbles
1914–1950s	Bakelite thimbles
1916	Price & Jardine formed
1916 November	Alexander Gibson's thimble patent
1917–1918	War Chest Fund thimbles
1919 September	Aronson & Co. silver thimbles
1922 August	Nifty name first used by Price & Jardine
1922 November	L. Orbuck Christmas pudding charms advertisement
1923	Hallmarking introduced in New South Wales
1924–1940	Stella Palfrey
1926	Royal Worcester kookaburra thimble
1927	George Palfrey died
	P.J.P. gold thimble
1927–1940	Bebarfald–Blue Bird thimbles Sydney
1929	Royal Worcester kookaburra thimbles
1930–1932	Bebarfalds 305 Little Collins St Melbourne
1932 March	Sydney Harbour Bridge opened
1933 May–1942	Nifty thimbles
1935	Gabler SHB thimbles
	Pall Mall thimbles
1936 Oct.–1942	9 carat silver-lined Nifty thimbles
1939	E.H. Price left Price & Jardine
1945 April	H.C. Jardine died
1947 January	Nifty trademark registered
1947 July	First Elfin thimbles advertisement
1948 February	E. H. Price died
1954	Westminster China opened
1963	Robert Herron began woodturning
1968	R.P.A. Matho-Dudare silversmith
1970	Dot Andrews' Paris Creek Pottery started
	Halcyon Days Enamels
1970s	Tor Schwank thimbles
	Batavia relics raised
	Ray Norman silversmith
1971 March	Price & Jardine sold
1973–1993	Caverswall China thimbles
1974	Crummles Enamels opened
1974	Spode China thimbles
1975	Lauders' mini thimbles
1977	Nerylla's Antiques opened
1978	Precision Plastics thimble factory burnt down
1979	John Trier thimbles
	Eric Car thimbles
1979–1985	Haley papier-mâché thimbles
1980	Robert Herron's wooden thimbles
	Melbourne Exhibition thimbles
	Embroiderers Guild Victoria 20th anniversary thimbles
	Embroiderers Guild of Western Australia thimbles
	Wedgwood thimbles
	Frank Cowan thimbles
	Irene Marshall thimbles
1980s	Westminster China thimbles
	Australian Collectors Treasury thimbles
	Whitehill Silver & Plate Co. Australian thimbles
	Christian Vocke's thimbles
	Keith Warhurst's copper thimbles
	Riccardo's pewter thimbles
	Perfection Plate thimbles
	Allan Davis' whalebone thimbles
	Ralph Bennett's ivory thimbles

Appendix

1981	Thimble Society of London
	Embroiderers Guild Victoria 21st anniversary thimbles
	Sutherland China thimbles
1982	Franklin Mint Baby Animals of the World
	Melbourne Quilt Exhibition thimbles
1983	Birchcroft Bone China
	Woodsetton Peeps
	America's Cup thimbles
	Daniel Jenkins thimbles
	Prince Charles and Diana's Australian Visit thimbles
	Yvonne Winspear's kangaroo skin thimbles
1983–1990	Thimble Collections
1984	Tony Bouchet's Agateware thimbles
	Franklin Mint advertising series
1984–1994	Syd Oates' thimbles
1985	Pan Arts 'Australia Series'
	Thimbella opened
	Pat Hagan's thimbles
	Exquisite Creations Adelaide Grand Prix thimbles
1986	The Thimble Collector
	Embroiderers Guild of South Australia's commemorative thimbles
	Vale China
1987	Needlework Tool Collectors Society of Australia formed
	John Tarasin thimble
	Agateware Bicentenary thimbles
1988	Pat Holcombe's thimbles
	Thimbleselect, Perth
	South Australian Digitabulists Society formed
	Embroiderers Guild NSW Bicentennial thimbles
	Liberty Lane QVB thimbles
	Pan Arts Bicentenary china thimbles
	Sutherland Bicentenary visit of Prince and Princess of Wales thimbles
	Expo 1988 china thimbles
	Woodsetton Bicentenary thimbles
	Woodsetton Expo 1988 thimbles
	Woodsetton 1988 visit of Prince and Princess of Wales thimbles
	Mark Models Bicentenary thimbles
	History Craft Bicentenary thimbles
	N. Parker's thimble
	Richard Ivey's silver thimble
	Brisbane City Hall thimbles
	Yvonne Winspear's Bicentenary thimbles
1988–1989	Impress Ceramics
1989	Curtis Hine thimbles
	Gallery One
	Australian Impressions series
	Pan Arts Signature Series
	Miniature Kingdom kangaroo thimbles
	NTCSA's fridge magnets
	Sun-Herald Koala Fund Thimbles
1990	Embroiderers Guild Victoria 30th anniversary thimbles
	Pan Arts WWF Endangered Species series
	Wedgwood pink heath thimbles
	Pan Arts pewter thimbles
	1st NTCSA Corroboree thimbles and postcards
	Pan Arts' pewter thimbles
	SADS' handpainted thimbles
	Pan Arts' Endangered and Threatened Species series
1991	Malcolm Walter thimbles
	Col Ward thimbles
1992	Bill Robinson thimbles
	2nd NTCSA Corroboree thimbles
	P G Enterprises kangaroo thimbles
	Sydney Sesquicentenary thimbles
	Ashley Downs' city thimbles
	Melbourne Quilt Exhibition thimbles
1993	Ian Hannay's thimbles
	Embroiderers Guild of Queensland 25th anniversary thimbles
	Lynn Richards' thimble holders
1994	Ian Trafford-Walker's thimbles
	Royal Grafton May Gibbs thimbles
1995	Kyneton China thimbles
	Moorland Miniatures kangaroo thimbles
	John Storm gold thimble
1996	Platypus Gallery koala thimbles
	Sandra Menger thimbles
	Ray Brittain thimbles
1997	CWA thimbles (Vale)

Bibliography

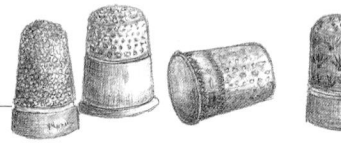

Adam-Smith, Patsy (1984) *Australian women at war.* Melbourne, Nelson

Aldridge, Elizabeth (1983/86) *Thoughts on thimbles.* Thimble Collectors International

Australian Aboriginal culture. (1989) Canberra, AGPS

Australian antiques: First Fleet to Federation. (1977) Sydney, Golden Press

Australian Home Journal 1913, 1919–1928

Australian Official Journal of Patents, vol. 22, no. 50 1915; vol. 24 no. 38 and no. 43, 1916

Australian Manufacturing Jewellers Watchmakers & Opticians Gazette. Melbourne 1906–1960

Bertrand, Christina (1986) *Brass thimbles.* Thimble Collectors International

Betensley, B (1980) *52 thimble patents.* Westville IN, B Betensley

Bloomquist, Lucile (1992) *A dictionary for collectors.*

Bryden-Brown, John (1981) *Ads that made Australia.* Doubleday

Cavill, Kenneth (1990) 'The jewellery of Aronson and Company, Melbourne.' *Australiana,* August 1990. p76–82

—(1992) *Australian jewellers: gold & silversmiths and marks.* Roseville NSW, CGC Gold

Commonwealth Jeweller & Watchmaker. Sydney 1916–1970

De Vries Evans, Susanna (1987) *Pioneer women, pioneer land: yesterday's tall poppies.* Sydney, Angus & Robertson

DerMarderosian, Ara (1986) 'Plastics used in thimble manufacture.' *TCI Bulletin,* January 1986. p1–4

DerMarderosian, Evelyn *Thimble language: a thimble collector's glossary of terms.* Wilmington DE, Dine-American

Erickson, Dorothy (1989) 'Nineteenth century silversmiths and goldsmiths (jewellers of Western Australia.' *Australiana,* August 1989

Flood, Josephine (1980) *The Moth Hunters: Aboriginal prehistory of the Australian Alps.* Canberra, Australian Institute of Aboriginal Studies

Frank, Beryl (1993) 'German enamel thimbles.' *TCI Bulletin,* April 1993. p1, 3–4

Friend, Dorothy Hess (1987) 'British commemorative and souvenir thimbles.' Thimble Collectors International: Addenda in *TCI Bulletin,* January 1990. p 20–21

Gebruder Gabler (1988) *Preise und Abbildungen von Gebruder Gabler G.m.b. H. Fingerhutfabriek Schorndorf (Wurttbg.) Gegrundet 1825* edited by Paul H. Jungbludt Trier, WVT

Gibson, I A S (1993) *British thimble size systems.*

Gilmore, Mary (1986) *Old days, old ways: a book of reflections.* North Ryde, Angus & Robertson (first published 1934)

Gowan, Susan Jean (1995) *Thimbles and other needlework tools: a selective bibliography.* Self published

Greif, Helmut (1984) *Talks about thimbles: a cultural historical study.* Creglingen, Fingerhutmuseum

Hawkins, J B (1973) *Australian silver 1800–1900.* National Trust of Australia

—(1990) *19th Century Australian silver.* Woodbridge Suffolk, Antique Collectors Club. 2v

Hearth & home: women's decorative arts & crafts 1800–1950. (1988) Glebe, Historic Houses Trust of New South Wales

Holmes, Edwin F (1985) *History of thimbles.* Dublin, Gill

—(1986) 'Nautical archaeology.' *TCI Bulletin,* July 1986. p2–5

—(1988) 'Thimbles from Mesopotamia.' *Thimble Society of London,* spring 1988. p3

—(1990) 'British patents relating to thimbles.' *Thimble Notes and Queries: Supplement,* winter 1990. p4–5

Huddington, John *Antique silver: a guide for would-be connoisseurs.* Pelham

Isaacs, Jennifer (1987) *The gentle arts: 200 years of Australian women's domestic & decorative arts.* Sydney, Ure Smith

Johnson, Eleanor (1982) *Thimbles.* Princes Risborough, Shire Publications

Kelly, Barbara (1988) 'Australian commemorative thimbles.' *The Record,* August 1988. p14

—(1992) 'The romance of the thimble.' *Antiques in New South Wales,* August-December 1992. p23

Landis, Alan (1996) 'Australiana on Royal Worcester porcelain.' *Australian antique collector,* 51st edition. p112–116

Lundquist, Myrtle (1970) *The book of a thousand*

Bibliography

thimbles. Des Moines, IA, Wallace-Homestead

Mayer, Wolf (1976) *A field guide to Australian rocks, minerals and gemstones*. Rigby

McConnel, Bridget (1991) *The Letts guide to collecting thimbles*. London, Letts

Mealings, Richard & John J von Hoelle (1984) *Charles Iles & Company, thimblers to the world*. Wilmington DE, Dine-American

Needlework Tool Collectors Society of Australia Newsletter. June 1991; May 1994

O'Neill, Vivienne (1994) 'Advertising and ephemeral sewing collectables.' *Needlework Tool Collectors Society of Australia Newsletter*. October 1994

Orders, D'Arcy & Richard Goux Stern (1993) 'Advertising thimbles.' *Needlework Tool Collectors Society of Australia Newsletter*. June 1991; May 1994

Pye, Cath (1995) 'Kyneton Fine China.' *Needlework Tool Collectors Society of Australia Newsletter*, No. 95/8 November 1995. p9

Rosen, Sue Pty Ltd (1991) *Historical outline Luna Park/Lavender Bay heritage study*. New South Wales Dept of Planning

Sandon, Henry (1987) 'Worcester thimbles—a few thoughts.' *Thimble Society of London*, spring 1987. p3–4

Sands & McDougall directory of Victoria 1911—

Sands & McDougall Melbourne directory 1862–1910

Sands New South Wales directory 1924—

Sands Sydney directory 1863–1923

Schofield, Anne (1990) *Australian jewellery: 19th & early 20th century*.

Sewmail, November 1997. p24

Smith, Babette (1988) *A cargo of women: Susannah Watson & the convicts of the Princess Royal*. Sydney, New South Wales University Press

Spicer, Norma (1995) *James Fenton: 1807–1886 silversmith and thimble maker etc.*

—(1997) *James Swann (& Son): maker of gold and silver thimbles 1887–present*.

Symbols of Australia edited Nimmo Cozzolini (1990) Coburg, Cozbook

Taunton, Nerylla (1990) *Collecting and researching in Australia*. Thimble Collectors International 1990 Convention Seminars, Louisville KY

TCI Bulletin July 1987; October 1989; July 1991

Thimble Notes and Queries. winter 1990; spring 1990; summer 1990; winter 1990; winter 1991; autumn 1991

Thimble Society of London. winter 1989; autumn 1994; spring 1995

The Third Decade 1980–1990: The Embroiderers Guild Victoria (1990)

von Hoelle, John J (1986) *Thimble collector's encyclopedia*. 3rd ed. Lombard Ill, Wallace-Homestead

The War workers gazette: a record of organised civilian war effort in New South Wales. (1918) Sydney, Winn & Co

Wendts Ltd (1954) *100 years 1854–1954 being the history of the jewellery and watchmaking House of Wendts Limited*. Adelaide: Griffin Press

Woolley, Iris (1988) 'Thimbling down under.' *TCI Bulletin*. vol. 5, no. 7, April 1988. p4–10

—(1989) 'Australian silver thimbles.' *Thimble Notes and Queries*, no 4, autumn 1989. p6–7; no. 5, winter 1990. p18

Zalkin, Estelle (1988) *Zalkin's handbook of thimbles and sewing implements: a complete collector's guide with current prices*. Willow Grove PA, Warman

Useful addresses

Thimble societies—worldwide

Dorset Thimble Society
The Secretary
Mrs Jan Mee
8 St Michaels Road
Bournemouth BH2 5DX
England

Needlework Tool Collectors
   Society of Australia Ltd
L.P.O. Box 6025
Cromer Vic 3193

South Australian Digitabulists
   Society (SADS)
23 Harrow Road
Somerton Park SA 5044

Thimble Collectors International
   (TCI)
Barbara Acchino
8289 Northgate Drive
Rome NY 13440-1941
USA

Thimble Society of London
Grays Antiques
58 Davies Street
London W1Y 2LP
England

Thimble wholesalers in Australia

Gallery One Thimbles
Box 292
Deepdene Vic 3103
Phone: 03-9817 6638

Pan Arts Importing
18 Spencer Street
Killara NSW 2071
Phone: 02-9498 5480

Thimbles by mail order

Sewmail
Box 154
Melrose Park SA 5039
Phone: 1800 806 572

Barbara Kelly
The Thimble Collector
Box 336
The Junction NSW 2291

The Thimble Guild (previously
   known as the Thimble
   Collectors Guild or Scotland
   Direct)
Thistle Mill
Biggar ML 12 6LP
Scotland

Thimbella
Box 63
Meadows SA 5201
Phone: 08-8388 3224

Thimbleselect
Box 14
The Gap Qld 4061
Phone: 07-3300 1107

Thimble makers in Australia

Adrian Graham-Rowe
Phone: 07-5463 7296

Robert Herron
Box 65
Riverside Tas 7250
Phone: 03 6327 1377

HC Metal Restorations (Curtis
   Hine)
Box 535
Balwyn North Vic 3104
Phone: 03 9857 5359

Pat Hagan
32 Miller Street
Unley SA 5061

Pat Holcombe
2B Goolman Street
Chapel Hill Qld 4069
Phone: 07-3378 6326

Kyneton Fine China
Wedge Street
Kyneton Vic 3444
Phone: 03-5422 3337

Perfection Plate Holdings
26 Mavis Street
Revesby NSW 2212

Marylyn Verstraeten
Meat Market Craft Centre
North Melbourne Vic 3051
Phone: 03-9822 3137

Col Ward
529 Broadwater Road
Mansfield Qld 4122
Phone: 07-3343 6288

Thimble retailers in Australia

Nerylla's Antiques
498c Miller Street
Cammeray NSW 2062
Phone: 02-9955 4230

Index

A.M.P. (Australian Mutual Provident Society): 68
Aboriginal designs: 58, 59, 87, 89, 91
Aboriginal scenes: 64, 73, 81, 90, 95
Aborigines: 11
Adam, Pat: 59
Adams, Keith: 89
Addaline Miniatures: 14
Adelaide: 14, 17, 20, 31, 50, 60, 79, 105, 115
Advertising thimbles: 52, 66, 67–75, 96–7, 100–1
Agateware thimbles: 62
Albany WA: 92
Allowrie Butter: 68
Aluminium thimbles: 67–74, 100
America's Cup: 51
Andrews, Dorothy: 14, 59, 62, 64, 87
Animals *see* Birds; Fauna
Apollo Bay Vic: 95
Appleby, David: 85
Armidale NSW: 73
Aronson & Co: 18–9, 20, 124–5
Artistry in Brass: 32, 75, 76, 99
Ashley Downs: 48
Auburn SA: 63
"AUSSIE": 19–20
Aussie Fridge Magnets: 101
Australia Series: 49, 54, 116–7
Australia II: 51
Australian Capital Territory: 49, 50, 60, 83, 115, 116
Australian Collectors Treasury: 48
Australian Defence Force: 77, 97
Australian Endangered Species: 54, 116–7
Australian Grand Prix 1986: 79
Australian Impressions: 49
Australian Red Cross: 65
Austrian thimbles: 67, 70, 71

Baby Animals of the World: 51
Bakelite thimbles: 70, 96–7
Ball, John: 57
Ballarat Vic: 75
Bandicoots: 92
Banksias: 51, 82, 116
Barnes, Tony: 54
Barnett, Irene: 63

Barossa Valley SA: 79, 99
Barrett, Peter: 52
Batavia wreck: 11
Bates, David: 75
Bates, Gill: 75
Beaudesert Qld: 92
Beaufort Vic: 38
Bebarfald–Blue Bird Sewing Machines: 68–70
Beechworth Vic: 48
Bellerive Tas: 91
Benjamin, Susan: 77
Bennett, Hal: 95
Bennett, Ralph: 92
Bennett, Shirley: 95
Berrima NSW: 75
Berry, Jihl: 13
Berry, Margaret: 13
Bicentenary 1988: 41, 54, 57, 62, 75, 76, 80, 87, 97
Bilston & Battersea Enamels: 77
Birchcroft Fine Bone China: 49, 53
Birds: 39, 41, 54, 59, 61, 65, 79, 87, 89, 91, 116
Birmingham hallmarks: 15, 21, 26, 39, 41
Birrell, Doug: 85
Blue Bird Sewing Machines: 68–70
Blue Mountains NSW: 34, 116
Blue Nurses of Queensland: 65
Blue wrens: 16, 39, 53, 63, 87, 89, 116
Bluff Point NSW: 61
Boan Bros: 70
Bond International: 49
Bond's Hosiery: 70
Bone thimbles: 91
Bottlebrush: 51, 88
Bouchet, Tony: 62
Bounty: 75
Brass thimbles: 11, 12, 74–6, 77, 83, 101
Breaddough thimbles: 61–2
Bridgetown WA: 59
Bright Vic: 48
Brisbane: 14, 20, 35, 50, 57, 65, 71, 88, 90, 93, 94, 96, 97, 104, 115
Brittain, Ray: 96, 97, 115
Bromet, Abraham & Co: 26
Broome WA: 99

Brunkhorst, August Ludwig: 20–1
Buckeridge, Mr: 70–1
Buckingham Pewter: 78–9
Buderim Qld: 37
Budgerigars: 39, 41
Buffalo: 64, 79
Burgin, Helen: 14
Burness, Kate: 116
Burnet's Jellies: 71
Burra SA: 76
Bushells Tea: 67, 68, 71–2, 75, 96, 100
Byron Bay Lighthouse: 40

Cabochon Collection: 50
Cambewarra NSW: 63
Cameron, Caroline: 61
Canada: 25
Canberra: 50, 60, 83, 115, 116
Car, Eric: 32
Caringbah NSW: 32, 75, 76, 99
Caris Bros: 20, 103
Cattle horn thimbles: 92
Caverswall China: 50–1, 55
Ceramic thimbles: 52
Chambers & Rowe Marketing: 65
Charm thimbles: 26, 33
Chelsea Girl Stoneware: 63
Chester hallmarks: 15, 21, 25
China thimbles: 48–66, 81, 115, 116–7
Chinese thimbles: 58
Chown, John: 50
Christmas bells: 51, 89
Christmas pudding thimbles: 26
Christmas thimbles: 81, 89
Chrome thimbles: 83, 98
Chrysoprase thimbles: 99
Clarke, Jim: 96, 115
Clough, Don: 65
Cockatoos: 79, 91, 116
Collins, Kay: 94
Commemorative thimbles: 33, 35, 41, 46, 49, 51, 54, 57, 65, 75–6, 77, 79, 80, 88, 97
Cooktown orchids: 35, 48, 49, 58, 79
Coolgardie WA: 103
Coombe, Judith: 62
Copper thimbles: 76–7
Corbett, Amos: 103

Cornwell's Malt Extract: 72
Corozo nut thimbles: 96
Corroboree 1990: 14, 88, 101
    1992: 97
Country Women's Association (CWA): 57, 65
Cowan, Frank: 32
Cowell SA: 99
Cowen, Jenny: 14
Cowen, Katrina: 14, 101
Creed, Nigel: 61
Crestmead Qld: 63
Crochet thimbles: 94
Crooks, Nancye: 14, 87
Crummles Enamels: 77
Crystal thimbles: 91
Cumberland-Brown, James: 92–3, 115
Curry, Fiona: 88

Dad & Dave: 65
Daniel, Peter: 52
Daniel, Rita: 52
Davis, Allan: 91
Dawson, Stewart: 15, 103
The Deeping Woodturner: 88
Delaney, Gerald: 59
Delarue & Co: 21, 24
Dettmann, Rachel: 53
Dickson, Elena: 94
Dorcas thimbles: 15, 20, 28
Dunkling, William: 103
Dutschke, Betty: 94

Echidna: 34, 40, 50, 63, 79, 82, 92, 116
Echuca Vic: 87
Elfin: 15, 16, 21–3, 32, 120–1
Elliott, Marion: 62
Embroidered thimbles: 94
Embroiderers Guild NSW: 41
Embroiderers Guild of Queensland: 35
Embroiderers Guild of South Australia: 34
Embroiderers Guild of Western Australia: 77, 88
Embroiderers Guild Victoria: 33, 57, 77
Empire thimbles: 25–6
Emu Souvenirs: 65
Emus: 63, 79
Enamel thimbles: 10, 24–5, 27, 33, 39, 41, 77, 83
Endangered and Threatened Species: 54, 116
Endeavour: 79, 116
Endisch, Elizabeth: 59
English thimbles: 13, 15, 21, 23, 24, 25, 39, 41, 48, 49, 50, 53, 55, 56–8, 61, 68, 70, 72, 75, 77, 79, 80–1, 97
EPNS thimbles: 27

Ettamogah Pub: 63
Exhibition Building Melbourne: 51
Expo 88 Brisbane: 65, 76
Exquisite Creations: 79
Ezywalkin Boots: 72
Ezywalkin Shoes: 72

Fairfax & Roberts: 23
Fauna: 34, 35, 49, 50, 65, 79, 81, 87, 95, 116
Fenton, James: 15, 21, 24
Fingal Tas: 48
Firehydrant thimbles: 64–5, 79
Flannel flowers: 79
Flavelle Bros: 103
Flavelle Bros & Roberts: 104
Flavelle Roberts & Sankey: 57, 104
Flinders Street Station: 50
Floral emblems: 49, 58, 59, 65, 77, 79, 81
Floth, Ruth: 85
Flowering blue gum: 48, 49, 51, 58, 79
Forbes, Tony: 49
Fort Pewter: 80
Foster, Lyn: 85
Franklin Mint Porcelain: 51–2
Fraser, Bryan: 32, 75, 76, 99
Fremantle WA: 11, 32, 48, 49, 93
Fridge magnets: 101
Frost, Stephen: 80
Fundraising thimbles: 55, 56, 57, 65

Gabler Bros: 24–5
Galahs: 64, 79
Gallery One: 13, 34, 39, 48, 49, 81
Gallery One Thimbles: 13, 57, 80, 130
General Store Thimbles: 52
Genesis: 32
Georgina: 33
Geraldton WA: 11
Geraldton wax: 35, 79
German thimbles: 24–5, 27, 33, 55, 68, 71, 72, 73, 75, 91, 100
Gertler, Peter: 33
Gibbs, May: 56
Gibson, Alexander: 77–8, 122–3
Gimbels: 81, 82, 88
Glass thimbles: 91
Gold Coast Qld: 37, 60, 102
Gold on silver thimbles: 39
Gold-plated thimbles: 81
Gold thimbles: 43–7
Goldsmiths & Silversmiths Association of New South Wales: 17
Goodwill Industries: 65
Gowan, Sue: 2, 14, 59, 92, 102
Graham-Rowe, Adrian: 53, 130
Grainus Oats: 72
Gramp's Orlando Wines: 100

Greater Newcastle Permanent: 100
Greschke, Bob: 89
Greschke, Margaret: 89
Griffith, Frederick: 25
Griffith, Henry and Sons: 15, 24, 25–6
Grossman, Peter: 89
Gumnut Babies: 56
Gumnuts: 34, 36, 38, 40, 53, 79, 82, 86, 89, 91, 95
Gunter's: 104

Hagan, Pat: 16, 33–4, 130
Hahndorf SA: 32, 50, 76, 115
Halcyon Days: 77
Hales, Diana: 34
Haley: 95
Hallmarking: 15, 16, 17, 30, 32, 47
Handley, Margaret: 86
Handpainted thimbles: 48, 52–3, 54, 56, 59–61, 63, 64, 79, 80, 81, 85, 86, 87, 88, 89, 90, 95, 102, 115
Hannay, Ian: 34
Hardy Bros: 104
Harris, John and Son: 38
Harry Ramsden's: 66
Hermann, Louis: 35–6
Herron, Robert: 84, 86–8, 130
Hickling, Margaret: 94
Hine, Curtis: 16, 35, 130
Hine, Peter: 50, 76
History Craft: 97
Hobart: 48, 50, 84
Holcombe, Pat: 35, 130
Hopkins, Sue: 79
Hordern, Anthony & Sons: 15, 104
Horn thimbles: 91–2
Horner, Charles: 15, 16, 20, 26
'Housewives': 77, 79
Humphery, Roy A: 21–2, 31, 119–21
Huon pine thimbles: 84, 86–7, 88
Hyde, Les: 35

Iles & Gomms: 83
Iles, Charles: 68, 99
Illustrious: 66
Impress Ceramics: 52
India: 25
Indonesia: 40
Ivey, Richard: 36
Ivorine thimbles: 98–9
Ivory thimbles: 92–3

Jade thimbles: 99
Japanese thimbles: 48, 59, 66, 79
Jardine, Henry Charles: 27, 43
Jardine, Jack: 27–8
Jardine, Walter J: 27, 29, 30, 31
Jenkins, Daniel: 36
Jensen, C: 104
Jersey thimbles: 62

Index

Johnson, Celia: 55

Kalbar Qld: 33
Kalbarri WA: 96
Kalflora: 96
Kangaroo paw: 40, 48, 49, 51, 59, 77, 79
Kangaroo skin thimbles: 93
Kangaroos: 35, 37, 40, 49, 50, 58, 63, 79, 80, 81, 82, 87, 89, 91, 92, 95, 116
Kedzierska, G: 60
Kelly, Barbara: 6, 13, 66, 85, 87, 130
Kennedy, Mervyn: 89
Kerr, William: 18
Kilcoy, Qld: 94
Kimberley Region WA: 100
Kindermann & Co: 70
Knitted thimbles: 94
Koalas: 33, 34, 35, 37, 40, 49, 50, 52, 55, 57, 62, 63, 64, 79, 80, 81, 82, 87, 89, 92, 95, 109–114, 116
Kookaburras: 46, 56, 59, 63, 79, 82, 87, 116
Kranz, Rod: 36
Kununurra WA: 100
Kurant: 101
Kyneton Vic: 52
Kyneton Fine China: 52–3, 130

L, Zygmunt: 37
Lace thimbles: 94
Lake Argyle WA: 100
Lassetters: 15
Lauder, Betty: 63
Lauder, Ian: 63
Launceston Tas: 64, 74
Laura SA: 36
Leather thimbles: 93
Leschenaultia: 58
Liberty Lane: 53
Lievesley, Tony: 37
Lipsius, Marian: 18
Lismore NSW: 57, 104
Lizards: 40, 79, 116
London: 21, 77, 95
London Court WA: 50
Lundquist, Myrtle: 24
Lyrebirds: 59, 116

Magnamail: 54
Magnus Goldring: 39
Malacari, Bob: 88
Maloney, Betty: 2, 7, 8
Manufacturing Jewellers' Association of New South Wales: 47
Manufacturing Jewellers' Association of Victoria: 16
Marble Bar WA: 99
Marble thimbles: 99

Mark Models: 80–1
Marquis Ware: 97
Marsh Arab thimbles: 12
Marshall, Irene: 37
Martin, Barbara: 94, 96
Mataranka Homestead NT: 90
Matho-Dudare, R.P.A.: 37
Meadows SA: 14, 62
Melbourne: 12, 13, 14, 15, 16, 18, 19, 26, 35, 36, 40, 43, 48, 50, 51, 55, 58, 61, 65, 66, 70, 81, 89, 95, 101, 103, 104, 115
Melbourne Exhibition: 51
Menger, Sandra: 88
Mesopotamian thimbles: 12
Metal thimbles: 67–84
Milner, J D & Associates: 56
Milton, Jan: 60
Miniature Kingdom Collectables: 81
Miniature thimbles: 33, 63
Mittagong NSW: 38, 42
Monstera deliciosa thimbles: 96
Moonta SA: 64
Moorland Miniatures: 81
Mother-of-pearl thimbles: 99
Mr B the Optician: 70–1
Mt Isa Qld: 76
Murwillumbah NSW: 40

Nally Ware: 97
Natal: 25
National Trust of Tasmania: 64
Natural fibre thimbles: 94
Needlework Tool Collectors Society of Australia: 14, 88, 97, 101, 130
The Netherlands: 11
New South Wales: 16, 17, 27–8, 30, 32, 38, 40, 41, 46, 47, 48, 49, 51, 58, 61, 63, 65, 70, 73, 75, 83, 85, 89, 97, 99, 115, 116
New Zealand thimbles: 49, 58, 98, 115
Newcastle NSW: 13, 46, 85, 100, 115
Niello work: 12
Nifty: 15, 16, 21, 27–32, 44–6, 101, 118–20
Nirex: 65
Nixon-Smith, Joyce: 37, 90, 92
Norfolk Island: 49, 55
Norman, Ray: 38
Northern Territory: 48, 49, 58, 90, 116, 117
Novelty thimbles: 78–82, 86, 91, 94, 95
Numbats: 49, 116

Oates, Syd: 38
Old Umbrella Shop: 64
Opals: 39, 46, 82, 89, 95, 99
Orantes: 26
Orbuck, L: 26–7

Orcades: 26
Orchards Watches: 97
Orion: 26
Orsova: 26

P & O Shipping Lines: 26
P.J.P.: 30, 46–7
Palfrey, George Henry: 43
Palfrey, Stella: 43
Pall Mall: 27
Palmer, Merrol: 50
Pan Arts: 14, 40, 49, 53–5, 61, 62, 75, 79, 80, 81, 89, 91, 97, 116–7, 130
Paperbark thimbles: 90
Papier-mâché thimbles: 95
Paris Creek Pottery: 14, 59, 62
Parker, N: 38
Parry, Graham: 79
Parry, Ken: 53, 116
Patented thimbles: 77–8, 122–3
Patina Craft Gallery: 87
Paust, Viv: 79
Pecheur, Frea: 87
Penfolds Wines: 73
Perfection Plate Holdings: 82, 101, 130
"La Perle" Perfumes: 101
Personalised thimbles: 98
Perth: 38, 48, 49, 50, 63, 65, 70, 72, 88, 89, 94, 96, 100, 103, 105, 115
Pewter thimbles: 78–82, 92
P G Enterprises: 81
Phillip Island: 52
Pick-Me-Up Sauce: 73
Pilbara WA: 99
Pink heath: 48, 49, 51, 58, 77, 79
Pipimenle, Riccardo: 82
Plant material thimbles: 95–6
Plastic thimbles: 77, 96–9, 100, 101
Platypus: 40, 49, 50, 63, 65, 79, 80, 82, 87, 92, 95, 116
Platypus Gallery: 55
Pokerwork: 84, 86, 87, 88
Porcelain thimbles: 51–2, 55, 57–62, 102
Port Fairy Vic: 77
Port Macquarie NSW: 89
Portuguese thimbles: 83
Possums: 40, 49, 50, 63, 90, 92, 116
Postcards: 101
Pottery thimbles: 62–4
Power, Trevor: 80
Precision Plastics: 98
Prestre & Co: 101
Price, Ernest Hawthorne: 27, 30
Price & Jardine: 21, 27–32, 43–6, 118–20
Prouds Ltd: 18, 97, 104
Ptak, Ahmed: 63–4
Pyrography: 84, 86, 87, 88

Queensland: 14, 24, 33, 35, 37, 48, 49, 55, 58, 65, 90, 94, 99, 115
Queensland Quilters: 55
Quilters thimbles: 36, 37, 93
QVB (Queen Victoria Building): 53, 116

Rafferty, J.J.: 73
Ranleigh Ware: 31
Regal Fine Bone China: 55
Registered designs: 25
Registration numbers: 25
Reidler, R.: 93
Resin thimbles: 54, 97, 116
Reutter Porcelain: 55
Riccardo's Pewter: 82
Richards, Lynn: 60, 102
Robinson, William (Bill): 39
Rockhampton Qld: 57, 104
The Rocks Sydney: 60, 82, 87, 93
Royal Flying Doctor Service: 65
Royal Grafton Bone China: 56
Royal Visit 1983: 51
    1988: 57
Royal Worcester Fine Bone China: 56, 104
Russell, Ken: 61

Schools' thimbles: 65
Schwank, Tor: 39
Scotland Direct: 14, 57, 130
Scott, Bob: 66
Scrimshaw: 92–3, 97
Settmacher Bros: 68
Sewing kits: 100–1
Sheepskin thimbles: 93
Shell thimbles: 99
Shipwrecks: 11
Shorter, Frank: 50
Signature Series: 54, 116
Silk thimbles: 94
Silvafros: 73
Silver-plated thimbles: 81, 82–3
Silver thimbles: 15–42, 118–20
Sizing: 15, 23, 31, 35, 98
Snake Gully: 65
Soergel & Stollmeyer: 68
Soho Foundry: 75, 77
South African Thimble Convention: 94
South Australia: 14, 17, 20, 32, 33–4, 36, 39, 40, 42, 48, 49, 51, 58, 59, 61, 62, 63–4, 73, 76, 79, 89, 93, 99, 100, 116
South Australian Digitabulists Society: 14, 59, 130
Souvenir thimbles: 12, 24, 27, 63, 64, 65, 83
Sovereign Hill: 75
Sperm whale ivory: 92
Spode Bone China: 57
Stack, Olga: 89

Steel-lined silver thimbles: 19–20
Steiner, Henry J.: 20
Stevenson Bros: 105
Stewart, F. & W.: 73
Stokes, Thomas: 18
Stone thimbles: 99–100
Stone-topped thimbles: 38, 99
Storm, John: 46
String thimbles: 94
String-covered thimbles: 78
Sturt Workshop: 38
Sturt's desert peas: 48, 49, 51, 58, 59, 79
Sturt's desert roses: 48, 49, 58, 79
Sullivan, Kay: 93
Sun-Herald Koala Fund: 55, 116
Sutherland China: 57
Swagman: 60, 63, 81
Swagman Pottery: 63
Swann, James & Son: 15, 16, 39, 41
Swans: 49, 50, 79, 116
Swansea Tas: 48
Sydney: 13, 14, 15, 16, 21–2, 23, 24, 27–31, 33, 39, 48, 49, 50, 53, 55, 56, 57, 60, 65, 66, 68–70, 73, 78, 81, 82, 87, 89, 93, 96–7, 98, 101, 103, 104, 105, 115, 116
Sydney Hall Mark Company: 16, 46, 47
Sydney Harbour Bridge: 24, 27, 49, 50, 57, 79, 91, 116
Sydney Opera House: 37, 49, 57, 77, 79, 80, 81, 87, 89, 91, 116
Sydney Sesquicentenary: 49, 116
Synthetic material thimbles: 97

Tagua nut thimbles: 96
Tailors' thimbles: 77, 86, 92
Taiwan: 50, 64, 65
Tamrookum Valley Crafts: 92
Tanunda SA: 42, 115
Tarasin, John: 39
Tasmania: 25, 48, 49, 50, 51, 58, 64, 74, 83, 86–8, 91
Tasmanian devils: 87
Tatted thimbles: 94
Taunton, Nerylla: 6, 13, 130
Taylor, J.C.: 105
Tenterfield NSW: 104
Thimbella: 14, 64, 76, 87, 99, 130
Thimble boxes: 31, 45, 56, 57, 102–5
Thimble Collections: 13, 36, 61, 91
The Thimble Collector: 14, 66, 93, 130
Thimble Collectors Guild: 14, 75, 90, 97, 130
Thimble Collectors International (TCI): 31, 90, 94, 130
Thimble Exchange Circle: 14
The Thimble Guild: 14, 39, 57, 62, 63, 81, 88, 89, 91, 130

Thimble holders: 91, 102
Thimble societies: 14, 59, 88, 97, 101, 130
Thimble Society of London: 14, 25, 26, 61, 71, 76, 95, 130
Thimblefuls: 83–4
Thimbleselect: 14, 130
Thompson, Jordana: 62
Thompson, Kathryn: 62
Thomson, Mrs Ninian: 98
Tipton, W.R.: 55
Tobwabba Art: 58
Topazio: 83
Tourist thimbles: 24, 27, 50, 52, 64–5, 80, 81, 83, 98, 101
Towler, Bill: 61
Towler. Margaret: 61
Trafford-Walker, Ian: 40
Tribal Man: 58
Trier, John: 92
Tupper, Sylvia: 61
Turner, Jack: 14, 59

Ullmannglass: 91
United States of America: 51, 68, 80, 82, 96, 97, 98

Vale Fine China: 55, 57
Varey, Yvonne: 13, 35
Vegetable ivory thimbles: 96
Verstraeten, Marylyn: 40, 82, 130
Victor Harbour SA: 79
Victoria: 12, 13, 16, 33, 38, 43, 48, 49, 51, 52, 53, 57, 58, 72, 75, 77, 87, 95, 115, 116
Victoria Jane Bone China: 49
De Vingerhoed: 93
Vocke, Christian: 63–4

Wales: 55, 57
Wallabies: 52, 87
Wallace, Ann: 53, 54, 80
Wallace, Dick: 53, 80
Walter, Malcolm: 40, 89, 91
War Chest Thimble Fund: 98
Waratahs: 48, 49, 50, 51, 58, 63, 79, 82, 89
Ward, Col: 90, 130
Ward, F W: 98
Warhurst, Keith: 76
Warne, Beryl: 13, 36, 61
Warwick Models: 80
Wattle: 37, 41, 49, 53, 54, 56, 58, 59, 79, 82, 87, 88, 94, 116
Waverley Vic: 103
Wedgwood: 57–8
The Wedgwood Collectors Society: 58
Weir, Paul: 37
Wendt, Joachim Matthias: 105
Wengert, Julius: 33